Anupama Kundoo

LOUISIANA MUSEUM OF MODERN ART
LARS MÜLLER PUBLISHERS

Supported by Realdania
Sponsor of architectural exhibitions
at Louisiana Museum of Modern Art

Anupama Kundoo

Text by
Edwin Heathcote
Anupama Kundoo

Interview with Anupama Kundoo
by Martha Thorne

Foreword

How can architecture help solve the social, environmental and economic crises that the world is facing? How can the architect be a piece in that big puzzle? These are questions that most architectural studios today are pondering, no one more so than the architects the Louisiana has been showcasing in *The Architect's Studio* exhibition series over the last few years. Some studios produce large-scale key works that help drive the trend toward more sustainable building. Others start from the ground up with basic considerations of how individual people should think and act. Is it possible, say, to reduce the use of the Earth's resources for construction by investing in another resource: human knowledge and intelligence? This is what the Indian architect Anupama Kundoo proposes.

The Architect's Studio has given us a look under the hood, at notebooks and models, opening a window into the architect's thoughts. What lies at the root of the architecture that we surround ourselves with, and that we will be living in, in the future?

Kundoo is the fourth architect in this series. She bases her architecture on what she considers the ultimate luxury in today's world: time. This entails putting more time into the process behind the architecture. Into the building process itself. Into the research and development of architectural method and artisanal technique. And into the construction of buildings without mass fabrication and big machinery. Last but not least, it is about investing one's own personal time in the architecture, adding value to it.

Kundoo works with time in architecture on multiple levels. There are the seasons, the hours and the days, the time of everyday life. Then there is the time it takes to create the architecture. That time is one that tends not to be discussed very much. Or perhaps there is too much discussion of how little time production ought to take. Industrialization itself is the establishment of time as a yardstick – and as a problem. How can we produce the most in the shortest possible time? That gain has led to the creation of thousands of mediocre buildings around the world, marked by the generic concrete of mass production. In her work, Kundoo tries to return qualitative time to the production of architecture – by human work and human hand, which naturally takes longer than machines but involves a far better sense of materials, detail, space and the building's relationship to the site. Looking at Kundoo's buildings, it is impossible not to sense that they are unique works, the epitome of site-specific architecture. As Kundoo says, time is one of our most valuable resources, because of its scarcity in late modernity. We cannot produce time, but we can let construction take longer and thus expand time. In Kundoo's case, construction is actually less expensive than if she had used machinery and prefab building elements. Although her analogue, almost contemplative, method will not solve the global housing shortage, we can still be inspired by her approach to time. The pace of mass production, and the consequently poor quality of construction, needs to be re-evaluated.

Another way to work with time involves the time that spans generations – the time before Kundoo, her own lifetime and the time after her. Having learned from those who came before her, she is teaching the next generation of architects, who will bring valuable knowledge into their time. Buildings outlive people, and what we build sets the framework for the lives of our descendants. Accordingly, Kundoo has divided her work as an architect into three equally important branches: practice, research and teaching. The three branches grow from the same tree. Her practice as an architect builds on her research into Indian building traditions and use of materials, and into future ways of living. Translating ancient techniques into a modern vocabulary in her buildings, she rethinks the potential of a more collective and sustainable lifestyle. When she builds, she includes her students in the work, while teaching at several architecture schools around the world. Her students will also be involved when her big Line of Goodwill housing project is realized in the experimental Indian city of Auroville, hopefully over the next few years. In Auroville, Kundoo herself was taught by her mentor, the French architect Roger Anger who designed the city's master plan in 1968. She later built her own house there, along with a number of residential buildings and some of the city's first administrative buildings. Today, Kundoo is the chief architect of Auroville. She may be the one who carries out the grand plans for the city that were first conceived after World War II.

This catalogue, published for the exhibition *The Architect's Studio: Anupama Kundoo. Taking Time,* presents a number of Kundoo's most important buildings, including the future Line of Goodwill project.

Edwin Heathcote, the English architect and architectural critic, introduces Kundoo's work, her method and research into materials and building technology.

Martha Thorne, Dean of IE School of Architecture and Design, Madrid/Segovia, and Executive Director of the Pritzker Architecture Prize, interviews Kundoo about her method, her relationship to Auroville and the exhibition's focal point, time. Anupama Kundoo herself is contributing her manifesto on time as an overlooked resource in architecture.

We are grateful to the writers for sharing their thoughts and knowledge about Kundoo's work and India's historical and contemporary spaces. Profound thanks to Anupama Kundoo for articulating her thoughts on time – an eye-opener for us, as it will hopefully be for the visitors to the museum and the readers of this catalogue.

We thank photographer and architect Javier Callejas and photographer Andreas Deffner, who have painstakingly tracked and documented Kundoo's work from the time of her earliest projects, and photographed specifically for this catalogue and exhibition.

Thanks to the students and professors at the Yale School of Architecture, the Royal Danish Academy of Fine Arts' School of Architecture in Copenhagen and the Fachhochschule Potsdam, who have studied future urban planning in Auroville and translated their work into models for the Louisiana exhibition. Thanks also to Transsolar KlimaEngineering, Amour Group and BauKunstErfinden for sharing their research on intelligent climate facades.

Thanks also to Professor Gerd Fleischmann for his collaboration on devising the exhibition concept and communicating Kundoo's work, and for his contributions to the visual and physical design of the show. It has been an inspiration and a great help to work with someone with such deep understanding of Kundoo's method.

Our sincerest thanks to Anupama Kundoo and her dedicated teams, in Berlin and in Auroville and Pondicherry, India, who made this catalogue and exhibition possible. Special thanks to Alba Balmaseda, Luna Bucherer and Paloma Fernández-Daza.

Finally, we would like to express our appreciation to Realdania for their ongoing support for *The Architect's Studio* exhibition series. These exhibitions confirm the Louisiana's role as an international communicator of architecture. It is our pleasure to add to the growing awareness of humanity's place in the world, our forms of living together, our dreams and visions. We are delighted to be working on this with Realdania, as our long-standing partnership continues to grow.

Poul Erik Tøjner
Director, Louisiana Museum of Modern Art

Kjeld Kjeldsen
Curator

Mette Marie Kallehauge
Curator

Freedom from the Known

By Edwin Heathcote

Wall House built at The Architecture Biennale in Venice, 2012 (p. 10)
The making of terracotta tubes for Wall House, Auroville, 2000
Handmade Indian bricks and Venetian bricks, Wall House in the Arsenale, Venice Biennale, 2012
Construction of Wall House, Auroville, 2000

You might begin with a brick. Perhaps a flat red brick that looks a little Roman, a little rough around the edges as if it had been through more than just the heat of the kiln but also, perhaps, a few thousand years of history. It isn't quite a universal unit but it's pretty close, probably about as close as architecture gets to a fundamental constituent.

When Anupama Kundoo put up a full-sized reconstruction of her own Wall House in the Arsenale at the Venice Biennale in 2012 any visitor could witness the conversation between the bricks imported from Tamil Nadu and the Venetian bricks of the sixteenth century corderie.

The brick is the mechanism by which architecture is extruded from the earth. It embodies the elements, the earth itself, the water which makes it pliable, the air in which it cures and the fire in which it hardens. They've been making bricks like these in India for about 4,000 years, Kundoo calls it the oldest mass-manufactured building material in the world. That brick is everything; a block of pure narrative compressed into a seemingly banal, almost invisible object tailored to fit into the hand easily. It contains stories about material and the soil, agriculture, built culture, manufacture, the act of building, about the colour of the land, the heat of the fire and the evolution of a unit into a something which has not been surpassed. It shows traces of the hand that made it and the heat that hardened it and, in its size, it reveals the dimensions of that hand with humanity inscribed into architecture at its most modular level.

And that is only one collection of stories embedded in the transposed house. If you were to have looked up to the vaulted roof you'd have seen a ceiling made of interlocking pots and another studded with terracotta dishes or beneath your feet you might have seen stone cut by hand in the same way it has been for millennia. But you'd also have seen reinforced concrete which tells an entirely different story about globalisation, technology, modernism and the seemingly unstoppable bulldozer of an international culture of construction built from universal components often poorly adapted for their environments and adopting standards set in the mid-twentieth century.

None of these stories are exclusive to a person or a place. And yet they come together in a house which speaks of what cultures have in

common rather than what separates them. The Indian-made bricks beside the delicately-curved bricks of the Corderie's Renaissance columns only exposed when the plaster crumbled away over five centuries suggested a remarkable resonance, that conversation of cultures of construction across the ages and across the continents.

Those pots on the roof and those terracotta dishes indented into the ceiling are, like the bricks, vessels. They communicate a way of thinking, a way of making and the intelligence behind adopting and adapting, an approach which takes a found object and culture of making and is humble enough to wonder how it could be used or repurposed to make an architecture of conviviality but also naive and arrogant enough to question everything about it.

Embodied Thinking

Anupama Kundoo was extremely young when she embarked on her career as an architect, "straight out of college," she says. And she acknowledges that it was at least in part her lack of knowledge about what could and could not be done and what was and was not acceptable that formed her practice. That unwillingness to be bound by any conventional notions of architectural and constructional propriety and a sense of curiosity which made her eager to learn from skilled workers and makers but which also unafraid to ask obvious questions and to mix global and local languages is what has made her work so intriguing and compelling. It was also that inquisitive and constantly questioning tendency which has made her architecture both so magical and so impossible to pigeonhole. Which is, of course, exactly as she likes it.

It's impossible to look at the images of the Wall House and not see an almost infinite Russian-doll set of influences each concealed within another. The more you look, the more you see. You can't help but get a hint of Louis Khan whose architecture haunts Indian modernism, in particular anything in brick. But Laurie Baker is there too, in the ceilings, in the details. And Jean Prouvé in the porthole openings of those concrete pivoting doors. A bit of Barcelona in a vault, even a touch of Alvar Aalto and Frank Lloyd Wright. And all woven through with that sensibility of the hand, with the skilled worker. There is an idea here that architecture is a collaborative process, not

Pierre Tran House, 1992
Construction of Hut Petite Ferme, Auroville, 1990 (bottom three)

only on site but through time and through history. If the contemporary education of an architect remains firmly attached to the idea of the lone genius, Anupama Kundoo's work is an antidote. It is an acknowledgement that we work together. That the architect designs, the maker makes, the builder builds and that these are not exclusive arenas. Her contention is that through the transformation of architecture into a global industry of parts and materials we are willfully losing the knowledge and intelligence of both architect and builder as autonomous agents.

The skilled worker is able to adapt and to improvise, to solve a problem on site through using embodied thinking, a way of making that has become second nature and which traces a line in its intelligence back through time perhaps thousands of years. In emasculating that intelligence through a system of regulations established at the service of a global industrial complex we are losing not only knowledge but a way of being in the world.

That is why, I think, the Wall House presents such a compelling case for a hybrid architecture. If any architect talks about traditional crafts, skills or materials, about local cultures of making and thinking through building they tend to get gently pushed towards a sub-category of vernacular and excluded form a (still) modernist mainstream. If that architect is working in the developing world – regardless how ancient the civilisation of architecture in that place – an extra layer of post-colonial condescension emerges. The kind of sly suggestion of ethnography implicit in an idea of critical regionalism. That kind of categorisation represents a profound misunderstanding. It becomes exactly the kind of accidental othering that has hindered and split the world of architecture between a Western canon with its body of theory and everything else. If that is compounded with the distortion of another lens which interprets anything in the developing world as either 'tropical luxury' or do-gooding non-profit work then it becomes almost impossible to see this architecture for what it is, a connected hybrid of thinking and making influenced, inevitably, by the currents and movements of modernity and history.

Architectural Laboratory

The trajectory is itself revealing. In the first project, an off-grid

house of extremely modest means for herself when she arrived in Auroville with no resources, you can sense the student set free, the joy in making and building and being released from the drawing board. This is a house built from the things around it, coconut ropes, *pakamaram* stems, a roof thatched from coconut leaves elevated on granite blocks. It is a house permeable to the air and the breezes and to the ideas of making which emerged from the forest. It is an elegant dwelling with a raised platform for a bedroom and a hammock in an alcove for a living room and one which revels in the freedom of impermanence, of release from architecture's obligation to endure. The services consisted of a lamp and chord which the architect would take from room to room as necessary and solar panels to charge it.

And then the sudden jump in scale to the Pierre Tran house, similarly concerned with climate and ventilation but, now working for a client, imbued with a sense of permanence and solidity so completely lacking in her previous dwelling. Both were experiments, both, Kundoo admits, research projects in which not all ideas were successes. She points to the more permanent house with its white plastered walls which later suffered from decay and fungus due to the local climate and says that it led her to rip the plaster off to reveal brick walls far more suited to local conditions yet less immediately prestigious. White has remained the language of modernity, a neutral membrane of supposed perfection – which of course had always been a lie. The early modernist houses were conceived in concrete but built in cheaper brick and then plastered over to achieve the appearance of clinical precision. In that cosmetic covering dwells an entire sub-history of modernism and its conceits and deceits.

All this work must be understood in its context, the strange, visionary city of Auroville.

Conceived in 1965 as "a universal city in the making dedicated to the ideal of human unity," Auroville is part of a wave of alternative, utopian cities which grew out of the 1960s counterculture and includes Paolo Soleri's Arcosanti, Lawrence Halprin's Sea Ranch, Findhorn, Rajneeshpuram and others. Its radical rejection of capital and its spiritual underpinnings make it an unusual place and one that appealed to a young architect keen to escape the cynicism of corporate architecture. Like all those other communities Auroville

Town Hall, Auroville, 2005
The Palace of Assembly, Chandigarh, India, Le Corbusier, 1964
Golconde Dormitory for Sri Aurobindo Ashram, Pondicherry, India, Antonin Raymond, 1945 (bottom two)

suffered from personal and communal difficulties but it has survived and it proved a fruitful and hospitable place to embark on that particular combination of research, experimentation and design.

Sri Aurobindo, on whose principles Auroville was conceived and after whom it is named, had form in architectural terms. In the 1930s he commissioned Czech architect Antonin Raymond (who had worked for Frank Lloyd Wright, moving to Japan to work on the ill-starred Imperial Hotel and then staying there subsequently) to design the Golconde dormitory for his ashram in Pondicherry. The elegant building with movable louvres and woven teak sliding doors kept the building permeable to the breeze. It would become the first modernist building in India and a place of pilgrimage for architects.

For the planning of Auroville, Sri Aurobindo's collaborator and successor at the ashram, Mirra Alfassa, commissioned French architect Roger Anger in 1965 to plan the new town and the key buildings. The city was envisaged, according to Kundoo, as "an embodiment of the collective consciousness." Anger, she explains, didn't intend Auroville as a utopia but rather as a laboratory, a place of constant experiment, "the city the earth needs" (in the words of Mirra Alfassa). And, although the Frenchman was extremely aware of the urgency of climate change and building sustainably he warned of "the green religion," of greenness as a goal in itself. Planned in a swirling spiral resembling a galaxy in the making, a froth of creation, it is centred around gardens and the spiritual centre, the gold-hued sphere of the Matrimandir. Anger already understood the difficulties the automobile was presenting for the contemporary city and set about planning a pedestrian city concerned to maintain a human scale and encouraging intimacy rather than alienation and he concentrated on generous public space, on the streets and gardens.

Kundoo, who set herself up in practice in Auroville in 1990, was commissioned to design a number of the key civic buildings in the settlement and it has been for her a place that facilitated a journey through typologies, a line of investigation into material, making, climate, place and form which resulted in a rich, varied and completely uncategorisable series of buildings for both civic and residential uses.

That focus of intent laid down by Anger perfectly suited Kundoo's own sensibilities, the rejection of the fantasy of a utopia

(which, she herself suggests, is something that can only ever be a work in progress) in favour of a laboratory in which, presumably experiments can be accepted to both succeed or fail or, more likely, to embody a little of each in their development. The search is not so much for perfection but for the possible.

The buildings she designed here are all experimental, often radically different from one another in form and language but they address common themes of climate, the adaptation of existing techniques and materials, the integration of found products and technologies and the creation of an architecture that can be built using local labour, knowledge and techniques rather than imported, alien processes and expensive materials which do not contribute to the local economy. It's critical to point out at this juncture that even if the architecture is influenced by local characteristics, material culture and making, it is not vernacular. Certainly it is of its place but if that place is visionary it changes everything. These are buildings that look to the future but do not ignore the past. Time, as Kundoo says, is part of the equation and buildings do not begin and end with us but are measured in centuries, from before they are conceived to after they have disappeared.

Space Filled with the Story of its Making

The Auroville Town Hall complex echoes the swirl at the centre of the city in its lobby. Its broad, enveloping roofs evoke Le Corbusier in Chandigarh but without the self-conscious monumentality of the structures that support them. This is an attempt to create a centre for the metropolis but not necessarily to dictate its image. The buildings are open and dispersed, set around a plaza so that the public space appears more as a football pitch with stands surrounding it and the action, the moment of real importance is the gathering of the people not the building itself. Anupama Kundoo suggests that her architecture attempts to soften the boundaries, to "orchestrate the journey from inside to outside", between private and public, open and closed. Walls are physically porous, galleries, covered walkways and courtyards appear as interstitial spaces between the private and the communal and open spaces are left for users and inhabitants to colonise as they see fit, to adapt to their own ways of living and being

Sangamam Cost Efficient Habitat, Auroville, India, 2003
Creativity - An Urban Eco Community, Auroville, 2003
Volontariat Homes for Homeless Children, Pondicherry, India, 2008 (bottom right)

together. This is often the central open space as you might see at the Auroville Village Action Group Training Centre which revolves around a circular courtyard open to the sky, shaded by the structures surrounding it and their shaggy thatched roofs. One of Kundoo's largest projects, the Urban Eco Community prototype housing is similarly built around a central courtyard with elevated access always and terraces to create multiple levels and scales of communal space from the civic to the neighbourly and intimate. In its mix of rammed earth walls and vaulted terracotta roofs over large voids it has both architectural presence and a powerful connection to the earth excavated to make way for it and reincorporated in its structure. The Mitra Youth Hostel shares the language of an open circular courtyard but is determinedly modern, with its coloured brick plastered fins it could be from Miami or Mexico City. The Sawchu, a community gathering place is defined by its reinforced disk of a roof, here the centre is covered, the perimeter open yet the effect is similar, attention is focused on the public arena, the plaza as stage for the city. You could barely imagine a group of more different architectures than these, influenced by mid-century modernism, by Le Corbusier and Pier Luigi Nervi and by local techniques and forms. The Sawchu with its slender floating circular roof is an experiment in using ferrocement as lost shuttering to optimise formwork involved in the construction of efficient reinforced concrete structures. The plasticity of ferrocement facilitates the moulding of concrete slabs and beams so that they can be cast in non-orthagonal profiles that significantly reduce the volume of concrete.

In the Sangamam Housing on the outskirts of Auroville it is almost impossible not to see hints of Kahn and Corb, fragments of the memory of the Maisons Jaoul but on a closer look the walls turn out to be rammed earth, reviving a technique of extruding the building directly from the ground, a product of labour, time and pressure. The roofs are of the same terracotta pots Kundoo used in her own house, one experiment working out leading to the beginning of a language of adapted, found local material. And then two housing projects which, on the face of it could hardly be further apart. The strange domes of the Volontariat Homes for Homeless Children and the white modernist grid of the Full Fill Homes. The former is redolent of the

utopian desert communities and architectures of the 1960s, Arcosanti mashed together with Southern Italian stone Trulli or even Pierre Cardin's Palais Bulles, a collection of egg-shaped shelters clad in broken terracotta tile and with windows of pipe sections but their genesis is far more interesting than even the eerie forms suggest. These are both kiln and product, the ovens in which their own materials are baked. It's a fascinating form of energy-saving technology, embodying the energy into its own fabric in the form of the clay bricks that are baked hard in the process. The house, Kundoo suggests, becomes a producer rather than a consumer. The catenary domes are beautiful vaults, elemental structures like the dry stone domes of the iron age in Britain. Womb-like and with an oculus at their tops to remain as a memory of the chimney it once functioned as, they become microcosmic worlds of the children, the most archetypal representations of the universe embodying the intensity of fire, earth, air and water that went into their making.

Those kiln-shelters could hardly be more different from the experimental, modular Full Fill Homes. Here the building block is a hollow, lightweight ferrocement box which acts as structure, finish and storage, a house built from niches, almost from empty space. When I interviewed Kundoo in 2014 she told me: "People define my work under headings: contemporary vernacular, critical regionalism, it's all so superficial. I'm essentially modernist. That craft thing is a bit overplayed. That's just what makes sense in that place, in the context of India with its craftsmen. For me architecture is about the negative space. The function of a pot is in its nothingness."

The pot, like the brick, has been a recurring theme. And so has that emptiness, which is, of course, at the heart of architecture, the balance between the container and the contained, solid and void. In almost every building Kundoo finds new ways to build, to create a material or a building block which does something more than just hold up a roof, a module which contains within it not only empty space but in that space the story of its making, of a culture, of the collision between modernity and history and the potential of emptiness to be filled – by scented air, by water, by belongings, by memories or dreams.

Making of bricks, in-situ, India, 2000 (top and bottom)
Making of lime stone, India

Making Architecture, Making Life

Architects often bemoan their loss of agency, the way in which their freedom to create is being eroded by construction managers, engineers, cladding specialists, materials manufacturers and dumb regulation. Certainly architecture is increasingly defined by its global supply chain, increasingly homogenous as a field limited by the available and the easily imaginable, by an image of what modernity looks like. But Kundoo talks of "freedom from the known." What, she asks in her architecture, if we abandon those norms, that industrial supply chain? Through engaging with a society across its strata, from supply and making through labour and living, this oeuvre points the way to a restoration of that agency, to the role of the architect as chief-maker, as embodied in the Greek origins of its name. But it is more than just making space, it is making society and making life. There is nothing more modernist than that scale of ambition. Yet her work also offers us the opportunity to see what is already there and to use it, to adopt and adapt the richness of techniques, materials and work which has been generated from the particular conditions of a place. The bricks, the pots and the chicken-wire framed blocks and all, in their own ways, materials which have emerged from ways of making which are attached to the earth and the elements. They embed and embody the processes and the efforts of human labour in their fabric, the traces of the hand and the tool and bake them into place. Ultimately the house does only what those building blocks do, creating an armature for everyday life.

The nagging sense of a loss of agency, of architects' status in society and culture being slowly surrendered is, according to Kundoo, down to society's outsourcing of intelligence. The regulation which governs increasingly global architectural and constructional norms represents a delegation of control, a lack of confidence in humanity's capacity to create. The fragmentation of expertise in construction, the heating and ventilation engineers, acousticians, construction managers, cladding designers and so on are all symptoms of that abdication of control and, in a way, all address problems that the culture of construction has brought upon itself through its complexity and homogeneity across the globe where the same buildings are expected to address radically different climates, cultures and contexts.

Edwin Heathcote is the architecture and design critic for The Financial Times. He is an architect and designer and the author of over a dozen books including *The Meaning of Home*. He writes for a number of journals including Icon, GQ, L'Architecture d'Aujourd'hui and the Architectural Review and is the founder and editor of online web archive Readingdesign.org. He is also the 'Keeper of Meaning' at The Cosmic House, the grade I listed former London home of Charles Jencks.

"We want too much control," she says. "All I want to do is to open the windows." When she begins talking about buildings breathing, about the porosity to the air and about the balance of climate, nature and air, it's difficult to avoid thinking of yogic philosophy, the ideas about the body in balance or what Kundoo refers to as "alignment." She doesn't explicitly refer to these ideas (although she is herself an adherent of yoga), perhaps because it might be seen as too cliched a response from an Indian architect, an overarching metaphor too far. But it is always there. "In my buildings," she says, "I try to achieve three things. First a sense of contact with yourself, where you can feel well on your own. Second the contact with others in which you can feel yourself in the community and third a contact with the habitat, with the earth itself, with the air, the rain and nature." In fact there are more, there is a contact with the material culture, the making of the architecture and the way in which those are both clearly connected with the place you are in. There is a sense of connection to a broader architectural culture, an acknowledgement not only of ancient history but of the impact of a century of modernism and its radical upending of everything that had happened until then and the creative conflict that will be possible when liberation collides with tradition. And there is the luxury, the luxury of time and care embedded in the fabric, of the perception of the changing of the seasons, the texture of material to the touch and the pleasure in the apparent simplicity and intelligence embodied in the building. And finally, the luxury of time, the knowledge that any building does not begin with us but is rooted in millennia of thinking and making. We spend our lives inhabiting buildings, understanding them as background and foreground, tool and shelter, body and soul and they outlive us like the earth itself. We leave our mark and they leave our mark on how we have lived our lives. Like the brick we are units, part of something bigger, fired by life, leaving a legacy in a mark on the earth, from the earth and, eventually, back into it.

Hut Petite Ferme, Auroville, India

Hut Petite Ferme is the first home designed by Anupama Kundoo for herself, just after she had graduated as an architect from Bombay and was travelling around in rural India. The process coincided with her personal journey and her quest for personal freedom from the need for permanence when it came to shelter. Hut Petite Ferme was inspired by the simplicity of shelters in villages mostly constructed as self-built thatched mud structures, as well as the more complex thatch 'capsules' she encountered in Auroville's pioneering years with their triangulated geometry, developed by the Australian architect Johnny Allen. The round wooden structures of untreated casuarina trees tied together with coconut rope stood on rough-cut granite stilts that prevented termites from reaching the wood. The upper floor was of split *pakamaram* palm stems, and woven coconut leaves were the roof finish. The bedroom, a raised platform, was tucked into an alcove, and a sitting-hammock hung within another small alcove. Two solar panels took care of the lighting and music; a black plastic bag hung outdoors provided warm water in the colder months, and used shower water to feed papaya and banana plants beside the salad and vegetable garden. Round wood, as opposed to timber with rectangular profiles, can be used directly after felling, regardless of its irregular shapes. A relatively young tree provides the same cross-sectional strength as a much older tree needs to provide an equivalent rectangular profile. Round wood construction provides a viable alternative for building with wood as a cultivated natural building material. She lived here during the first decade of her architectural practice, and the experience had a profound effect on her holistic design approach, which looked at the life cycle of buildings and reviewed climatic comfort strategies – spending resources judiciously and looking for beauty in simplicity.

Hut Petite Ferme, 1990
Auroville, India
100 m^2

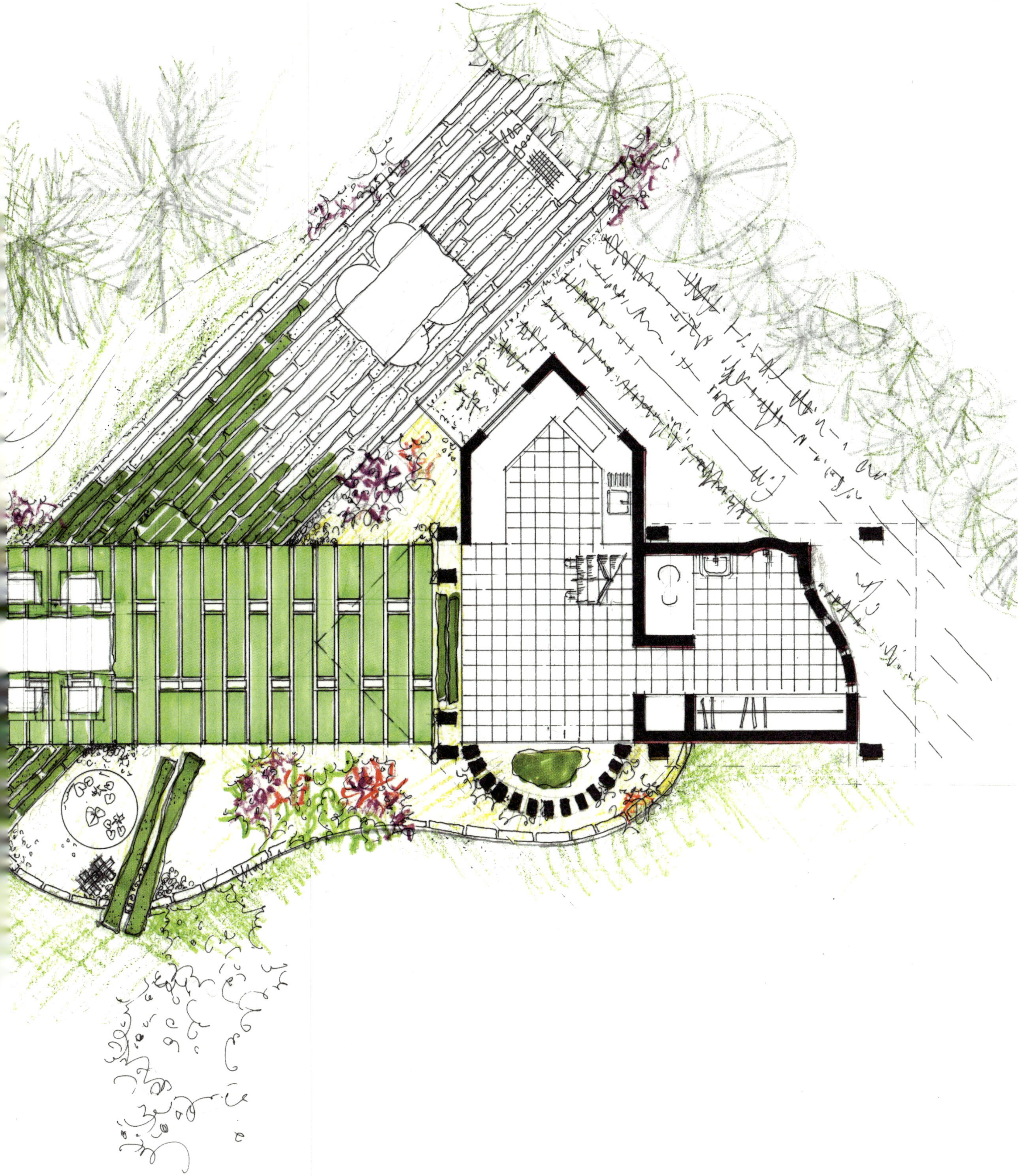

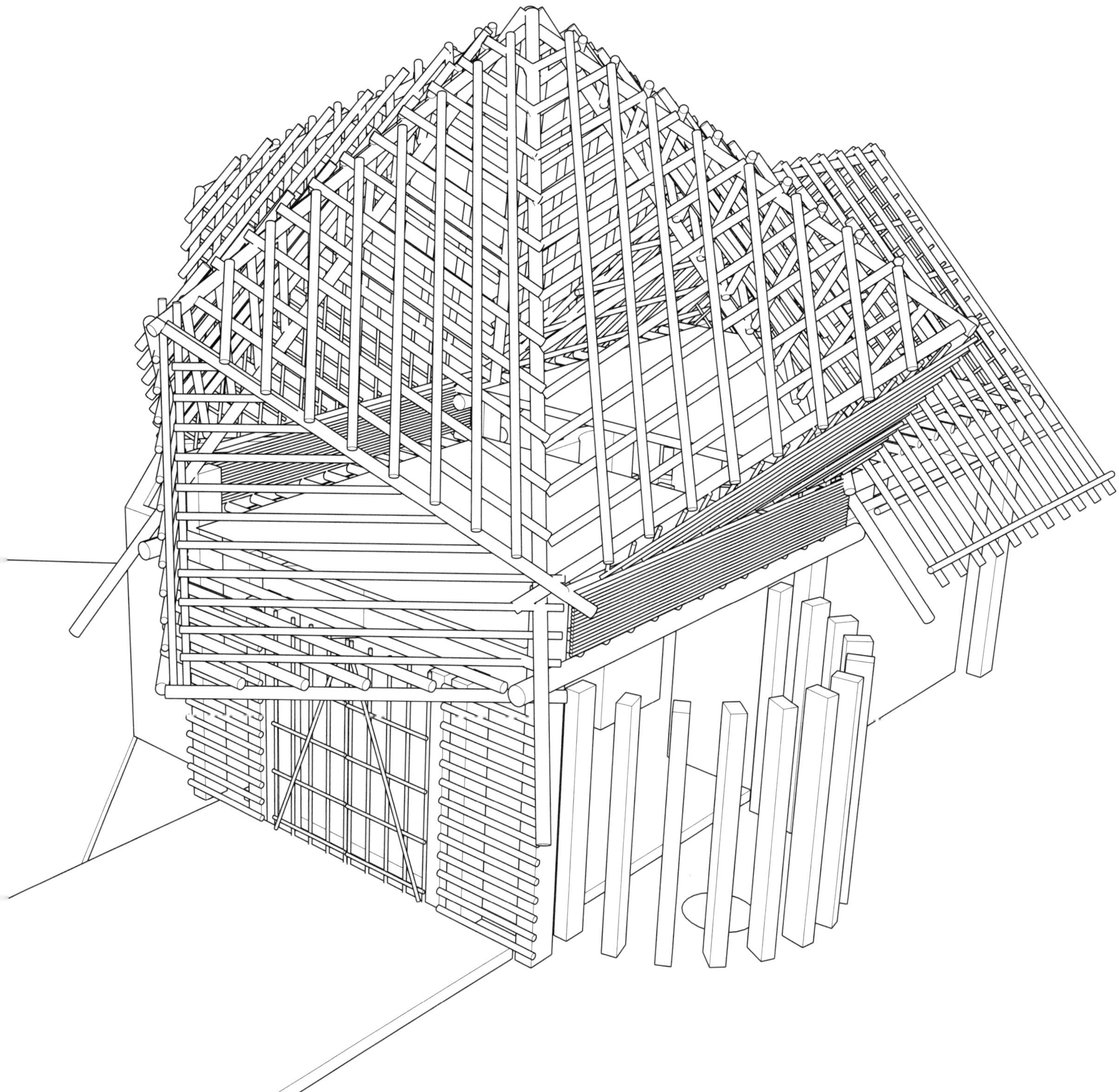

The hut was inspired by the simplicity of the village shelter as well as the complex thatch 'capsules' with their triangulated geometry is developed with the inspiration by Johnny Allen, an Australian architect influenced by Buckminster Fuller.

Wall House, Auroville, India

Wall House, Kundoo's own residence, is situated outside the city of Auroville, in any three of them support for the table area designated for research and experimentation. It has become a prototype for her later work. A long, vaulted space within the brick masonry, 2.2 metres in width, accommodates the various activities arranged in a row. The linear space spills over to the north east into alcoves and projections, and on the south west under the large overhang of the main vaulted roof. The design of the house ensures that the activities are cocooned into private secure spaces, while living areas are open to nature, where boundaries between inside and outside are dissolved. After living in the simple Hut Petite Ferme, Kundoo decided to avoid the most conventional building technologies, which are costly, energy-intensive and exclude local craftsmen. Instead Kundoo began investigating preindustrial *achakal* bricks and lime mortar that were still being produced locally. She developed various terracotta roofing systems that could provide a livelihood for local potters who had to compete with the growing metal and plastic industry. Negotiating the balance between hi-tech and low-tech, between handmade and machine-made, these hybrid technologies focus on new ways of using age-old local materials. The exposed masonry of bricks set in lime mortar is scaled down by the 2.5-centimetre thick *achakal* bricks, which require far less energy to make than factory bricks. Catenary vaults using custom-made hollow clay tubes insulate and eliminate the need for structural steel. Vaults in the ground floor use *achakal* bricks structurally. Flat terraces use custom-made trapezoid modules over partly pre-cast beams as in a jack arch. Terracotta pots are used as fillers on intermediate floors to increase the effective depth of concrete while minimising the volume of concrete and steel. The double height volume of the house enhances the air stack movement and increases the draft of natural ventilation.

Wall House, 2000
Auroville, Tamil Nadu, India
226 m²

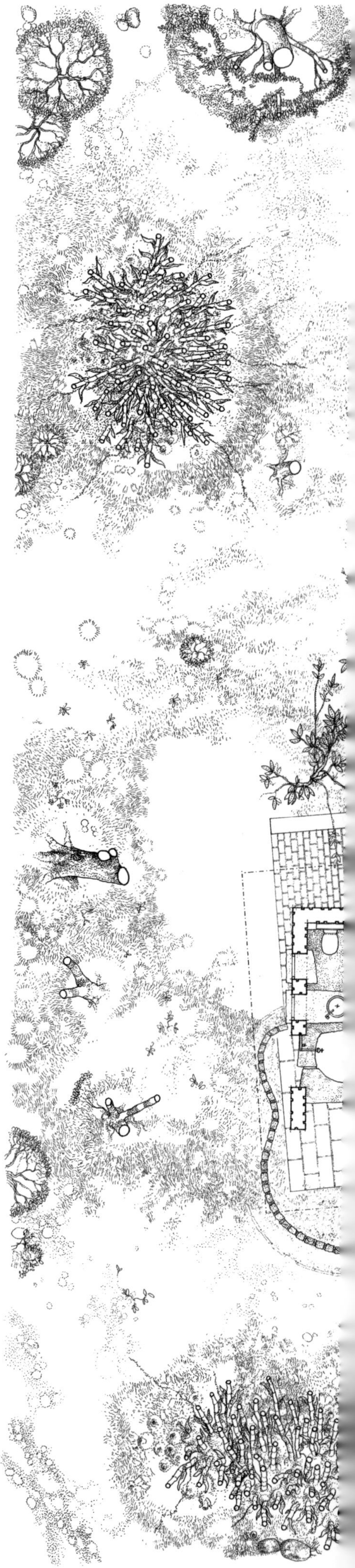

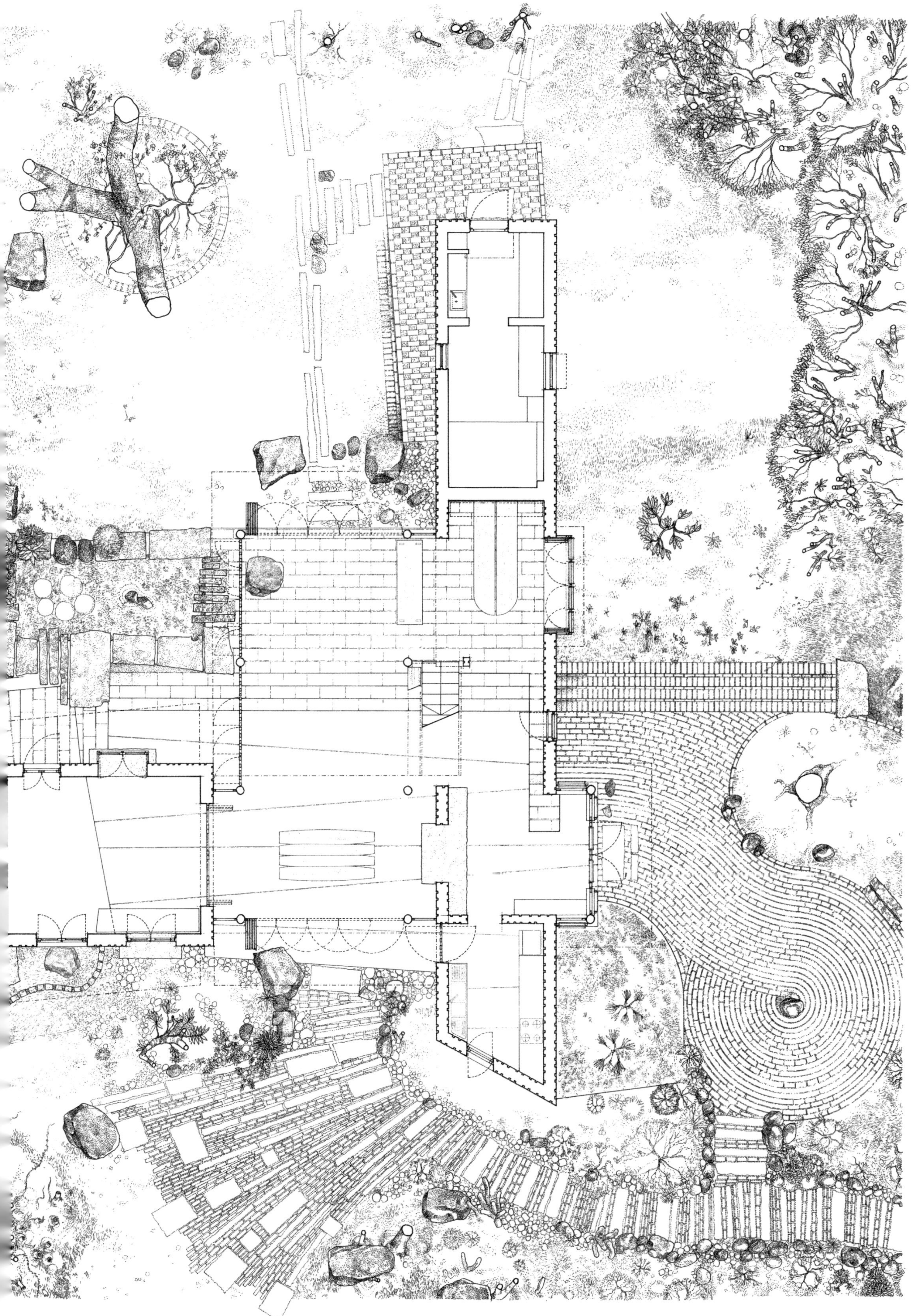

The flat terraced roof over the guest room has been built using hollow, extruded, trapezoidal fired-clay modules over partly pre-cast beams as in a jack arch, which have been specially manufactured locally in order to create insulated roofing solutions for flat roofs. The reduced energy requirements of the whole house were entirely met by solar photovoltaics for electricity, a solar water heater and a solar pump for the water supply.

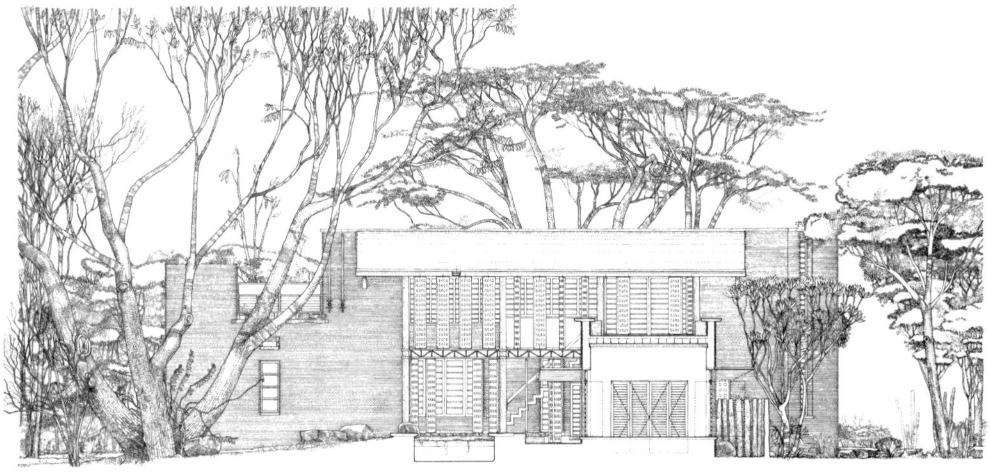

Landscape design, an inseparable part of the overall architecture, plays with the topography to integrate the indoor-outdoor transition as an integral experience.

The indoor-outdoor transition is accentuated in the semi outdoor bathroom, using natural rocks from the area as stepping stones.

The double height of the house enhances air stack circulation and increases the ventilation draft. Catenary vaults using hollow clay tubes have been used for climatic insulation and to reduce the unnecessary use of steel in *pucca* roofs. There are vaults on the ground floor where *achakal* bricks are used structurally.

Volontariat Homes for Homeless Children, Pondicherry, India

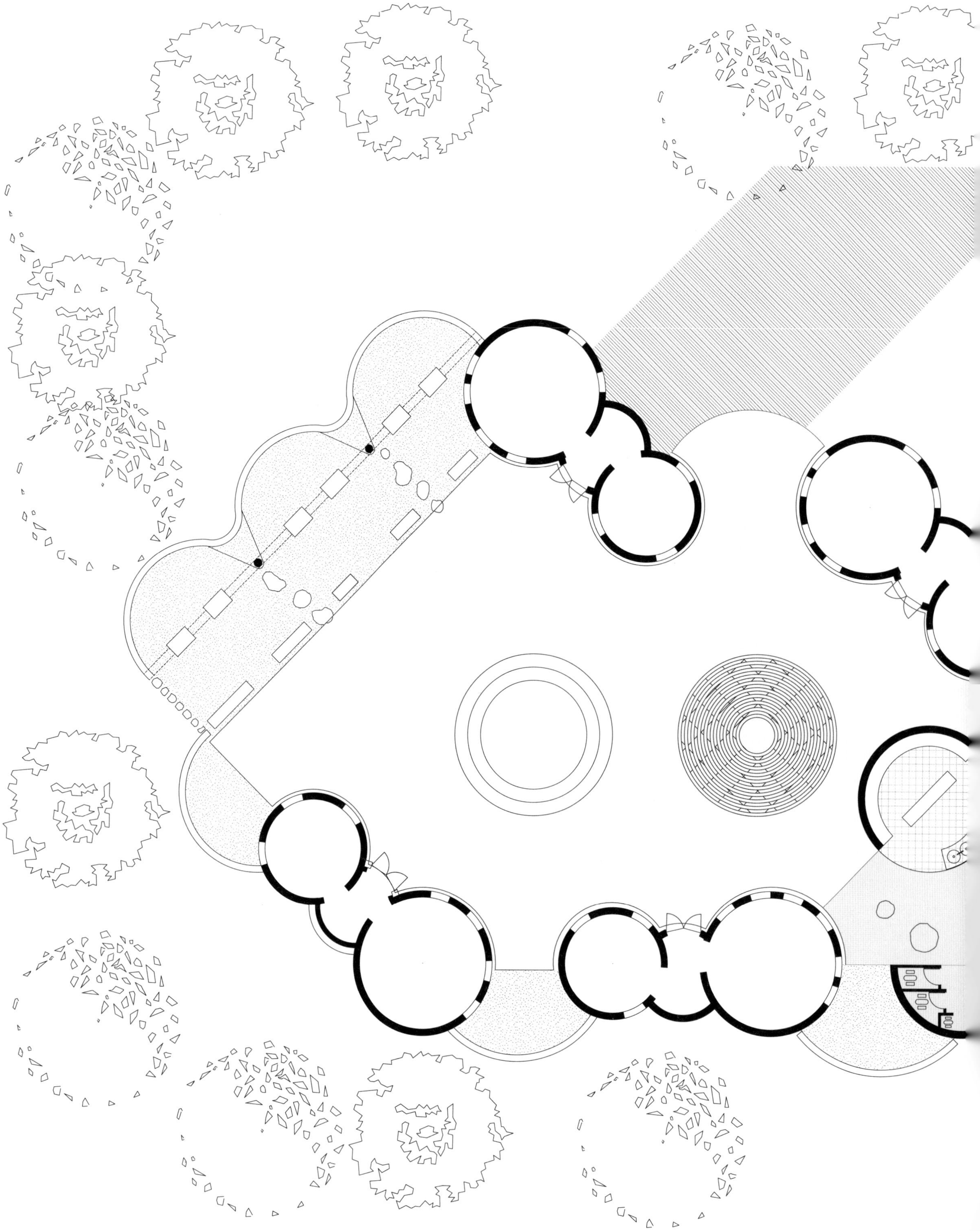

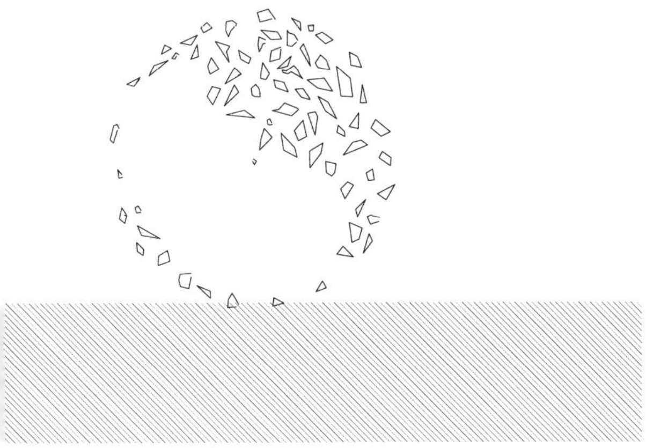

The residential cluster of homes was conceived to shelter children from challenged backgrounds as managed by the NGO Volontariat based in Pondicherry. Conceived as a fired-in-situ mud structure, the architect had been closely following the rare technology pioneered by ceramist Ray Meeker, which consisted of constructing mud houses and later firing them in-situ to convert them into ceramic structures. The onsite soil in the area was optimum for making fired bricks: in principle a structure built with mud bricks and mud mortar is stuffed with other ceramic products as if it were a kiln and fired for three to four days to achieve the strength of brick. Typically kiln walls absorb about 40 per cent of the heat generated. In this technology, the house is the kiln, and the 'heat loss' is directed towards firing the house and stabilising it against potential water damage. This technology is labour-intensive with extraordinarily little need for 'purchased' materials. The money spent thus remains in the local economy. The house becomes a producer instead of a consumer of sustainable building materials. The housing units were designed as inverted catenary domes that made direct contact with the ground, eliminating the need for walls entirely. Catenary-shaped domes provide maximum structural stability before firing when the structure acts as an earth building during firing, i.e. at an unstable stage of the vitrification process, and after firing as a brick load-bearing structure. Cost being a major constraint, the project uses absorbed urban waste wherever possible rather than buying building materials. Bicycle-wheel frames procured from junk markets were used as formwork for windows and later as window grilles. Glass bottles were used as structural units for masonry in toilet areas. Glass chai cups were used to finish the openings at the top of the dome. The project rethinks affordability in the light of sustainability.

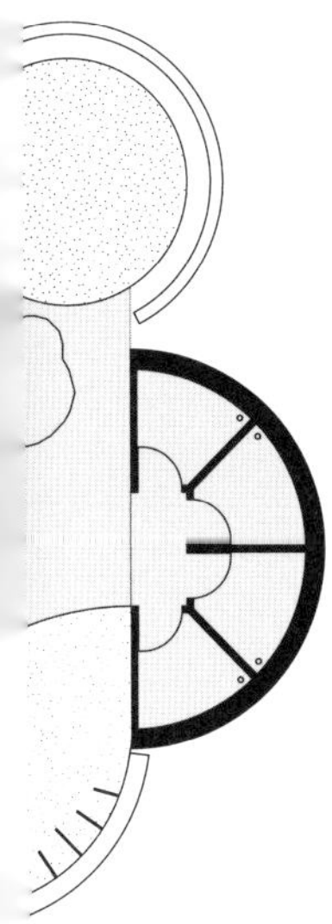

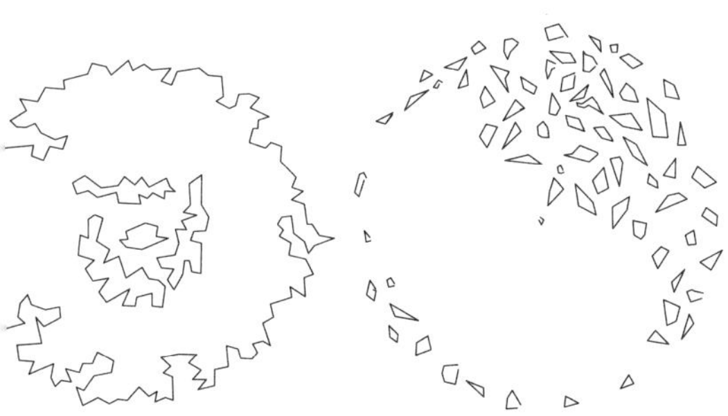

Volontariat Homes for Homeless Children, 2008
Tuttipakam, Pondicherry, India
512 m²

The domes are of various sizes according to the cluster programme, which includes one foster parent per four children. A social project with cost as a major aspect behind design, the project uses many unconventional materials and absorbs urban waste.

Bicycle wheel frames were used as formwork for windows and later as window grills.

The site is in a farmland where rice and other organic produce are being grown by the NGO due to the fertile black cotton soil. The onsite soil in the area was optimum for making burnt bricks and based on the architects experience with baked-in-situ mud construction technology, it was considered the appropriate technology to construct the low cost housing complex.

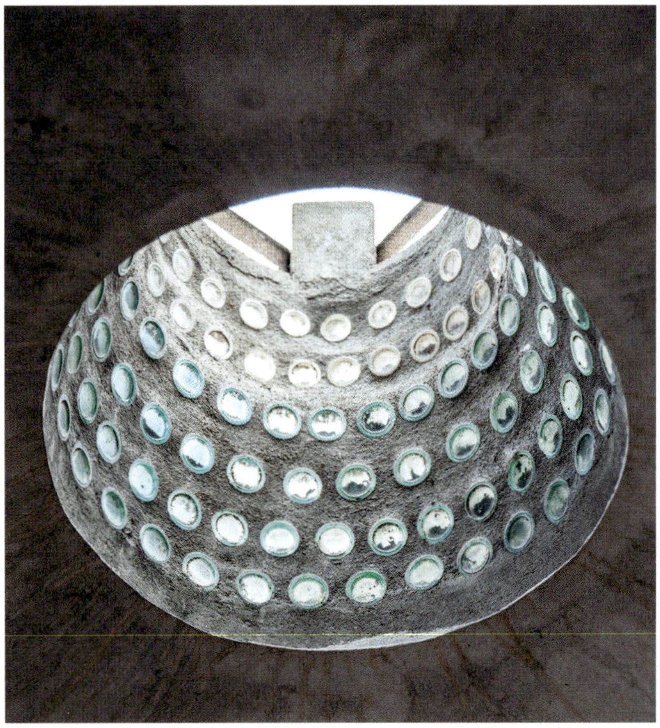

Glass bottles were used as structural units for masonry in toilet areas.
Glass chai cups were used to finish the openings at the top of the dome.

Terracotta pots are embedded in the central connecting dome made of ferrocement. These serve as individual 'locker spaces' for the children's precious personal belongings.

The entrance lobby that connects two earthen domes is connected by 2.5 centimetres of thick ferrocement and finished with a mosaic surface of broken ceramic tiles.

Residence Spirit Sense (drawing) and a small adjacent pottery (pictures) constructed in 2000 were Kundoo's first projects in baked-in-situ earth construction. The open questions she encountered led to her PhD on this topic and the further research that was undertaken eight years later in the Volontariat Homes for Homeless Children.

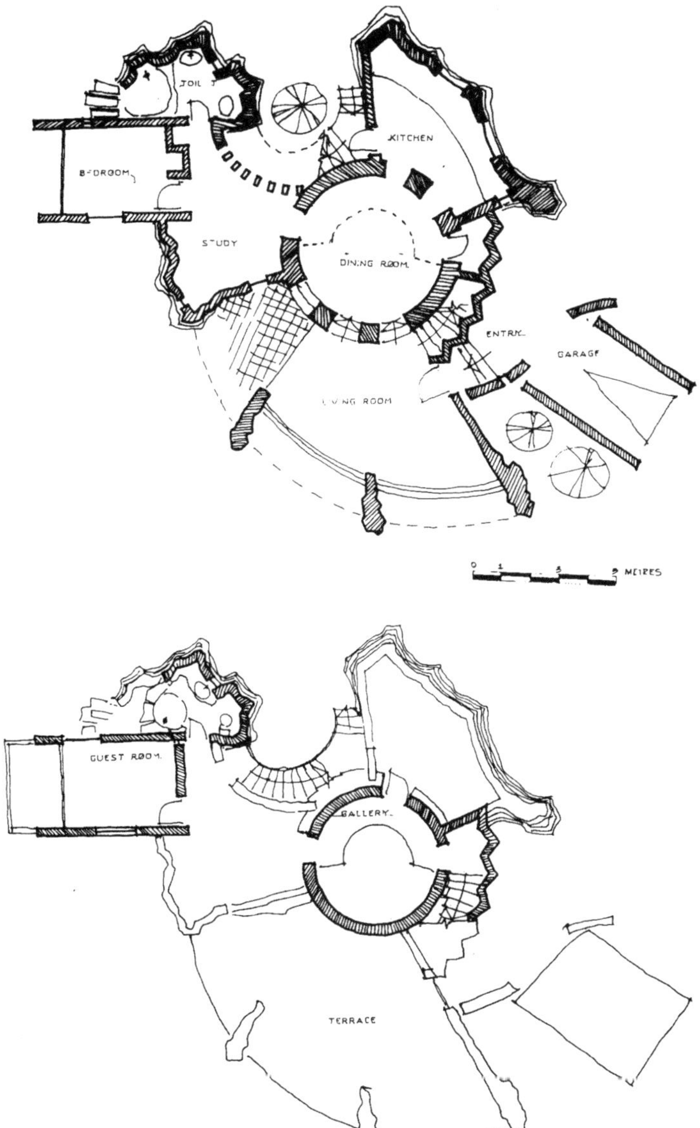

FIRED HOUSE ~ SPIRITSENSE

FIRED HOUSE – SPIRIT SENSE

Residence Kranti Kanade, Pune, India

The central idea was to work with levels, creating series of steps in the interior spaces that continue into the exterior landscape, to blend the edges between indoors and outdoors while creating a sense of expansion through the cascading steps. Through a central narrow water body that seems to cross through the house, and an adjacent double-height veranda space providing a range of volumes, porosity is achieved in the interiors with the illusion of a much larger presence of nature as the central experience, despite the function of the building as an urban residence. The large roof overhang, covering entire streetscape passages and verandas, acts like a large umbrella. Instead of covering each window, balcony and veranda with sun shading and water-protective projections, one single roof stretches over the whole residence and protects it from harsh sun and heavy rain. The various bedrooms are arranged to have cross-ventilation and independence from one another, and yet are strongly connected through street-like open spaces that expand into balconies and terraces. These different seating areas are used according to the changing light conditions of the day and the seasons. Outdoor vistas are aligned to flow through key living and dining spaces, with windows allowing transparency at either end of the axis which constantly leads to the landscaped exteriors at each end. Verandas and terraces on various levels and long cascading steps along water bodies encourage the interior activities to spill over into transition spaces between inside and outside. The structure is made of exposed brick masonry interspersed with plastered surfaces and a reinforced concrete roof. The Residence Kranti Kanade inconspicuously merges into its immediate surroundings and creates a sense of the outdoors coming indoors despite the compact urban context of the site.

Residence Kranti Kanade, 2003
Pune, India
502 m²

Apart from rooms for the owner – a filmmaker – his future family and his mother's room, there were to be workspaces, spaces for film screenings and other audio-visual activities as well as residential spaces for visiting artists.

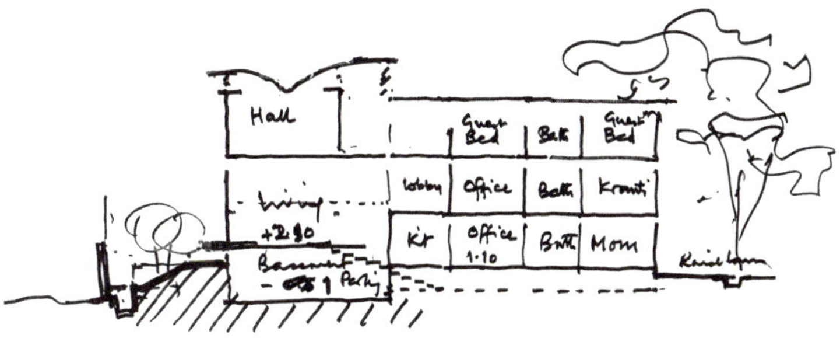
Hall
Guest Bed
Bath
Guest Bed
Lobby
Office
Bath
Kranti
+2.10
Kit
Office
1.10
Bath
Mom

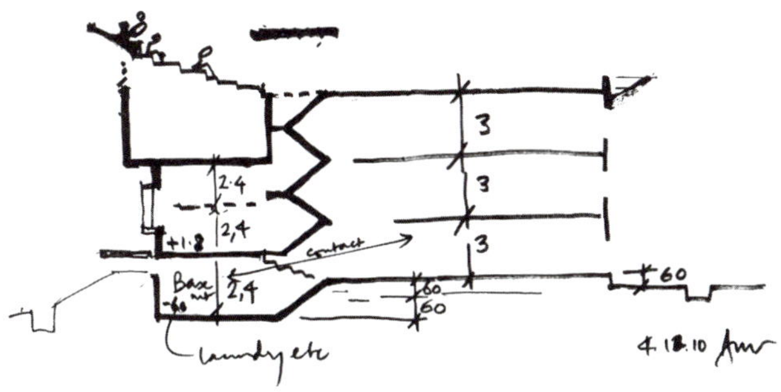
3
3
3
2.4
2,4
+1.8
Basement
2,4
60
60
60
laundry etc
4.12.10

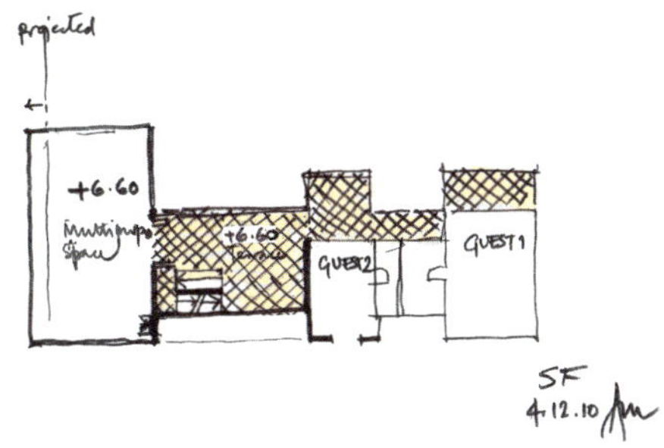
projected
+6.60
+6.60
GUEST2
GUEST1
SF
4.12.10

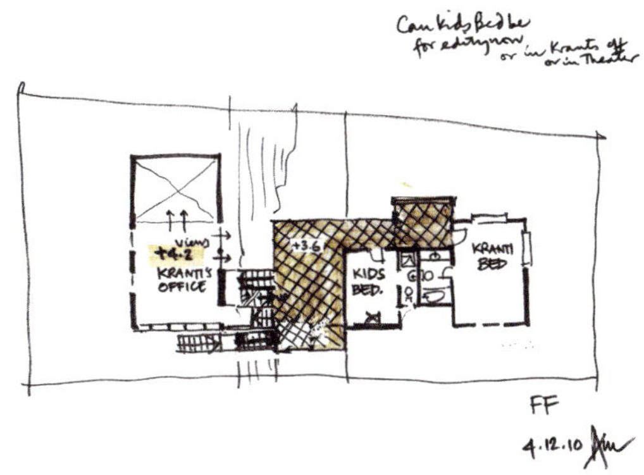
+4.2
KRANTI'S OFFICE
+3.6
KIDS BED
KRANTI BED
FF
4.12.10

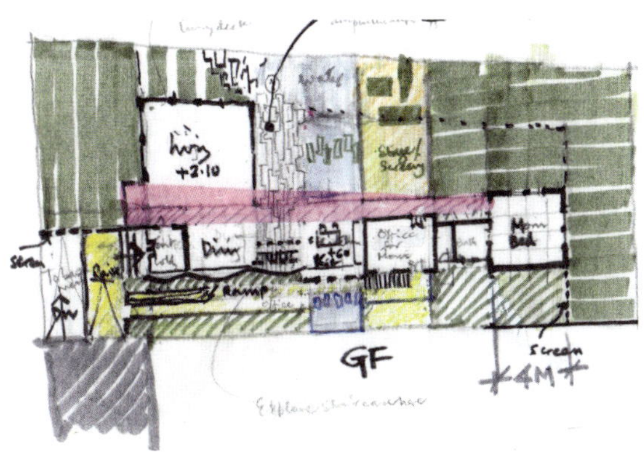
Living
+2.10
Kit
Mom Bed
Ramp
GF
Screen
4M

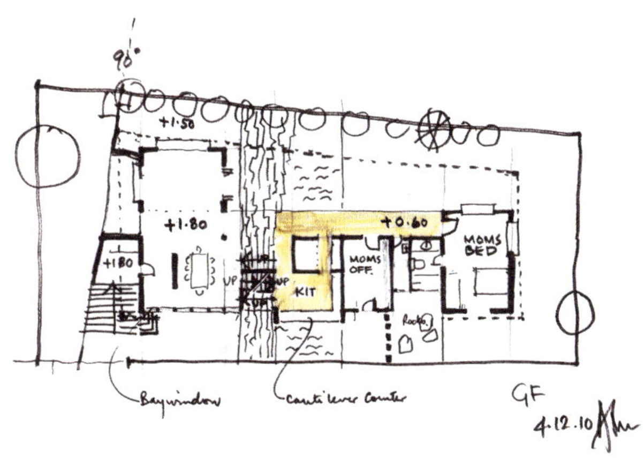
90°
+1.50
+1.80
+1.80
+0.60
MOMS BED
MOMS OFF.
KIT
UP
Baywindow
Cantilever Counter
GF
4.12.10

Shah Houses, Brahmangarh, India

Natural basalt stone was chosen as the primary locally available building material and combined with handmade hollow terracotta tubes for vaulted roofs as already used in the Wall House, given the proximity to local potters in the region. Apart from the main residences, the site includes collective shared buildings, accommodating caretakers' residences merged within the design of the compound wall in stone masonry, and a cylindrical water tank, also in masonry. The residences themselves are volumes in solid masonry interspersed with vaulted volumes that are visually more transparent. The vaults span the spaces between the solid stone masses. The lower vaulted areas are used for the social spaces such as living and dining areas, while private areas are accommodated within the stone walls. This strategy permits a continuous view of the waterfront through the different axes of the house from areas located higher up in the sloping terrain. The ground floor spaces are contoured to hug the sloping site with sequences of steps that cascade along the territory and continue through the house into the immediate exteriors. As a contrast to the natural colours and textures of the key materials of terracotta and basalt stone, selected plastered surfaces and floors are coloured with oxides.

Shah Houses, 2003
Brahmangarh, India
253 m^2

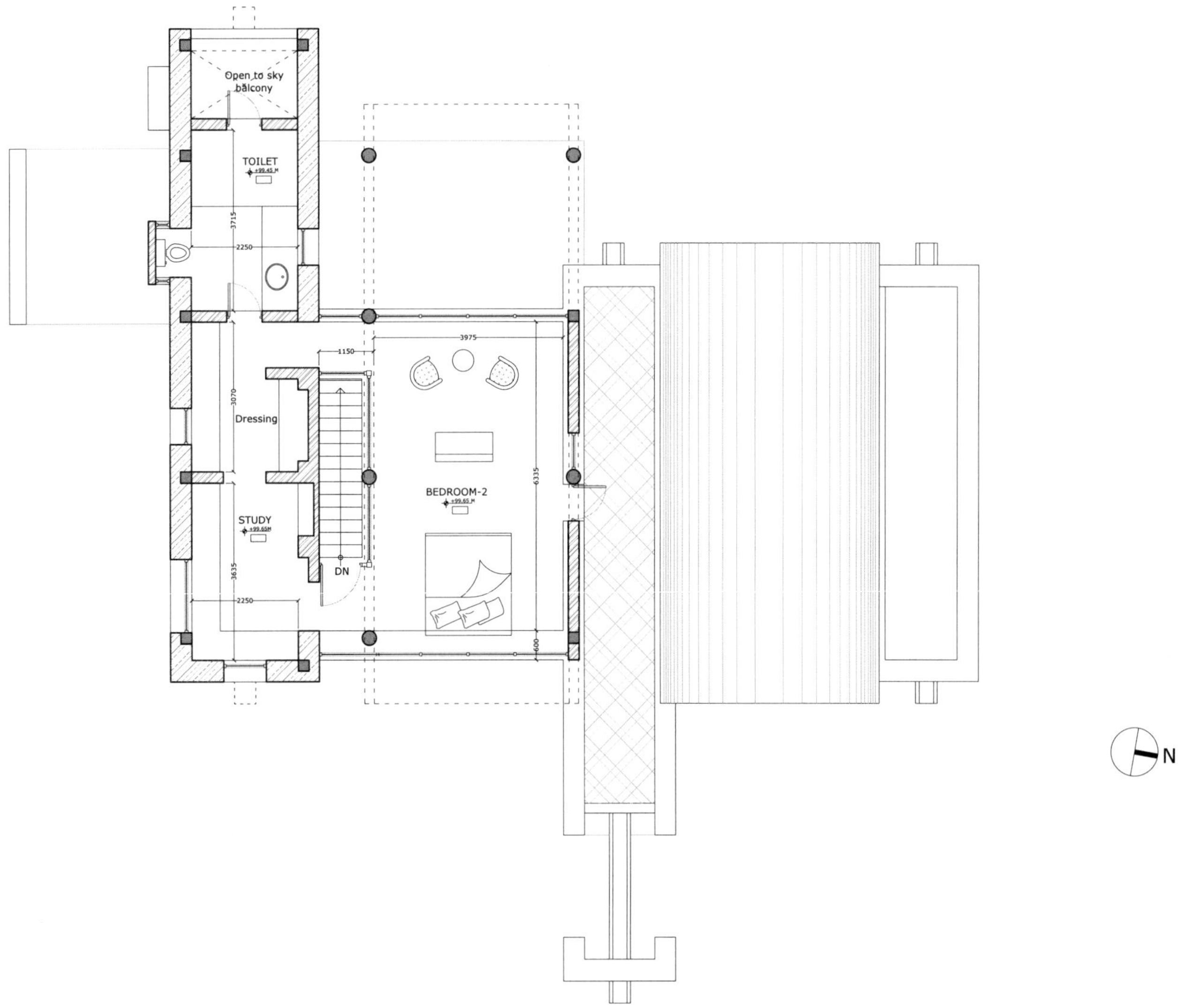
Open to sky balcony
TOILET
3715
2250
1150
3975
Dressing
3070
BEDROOM-2
6335
STUDY
DN
3635
2250
600
N

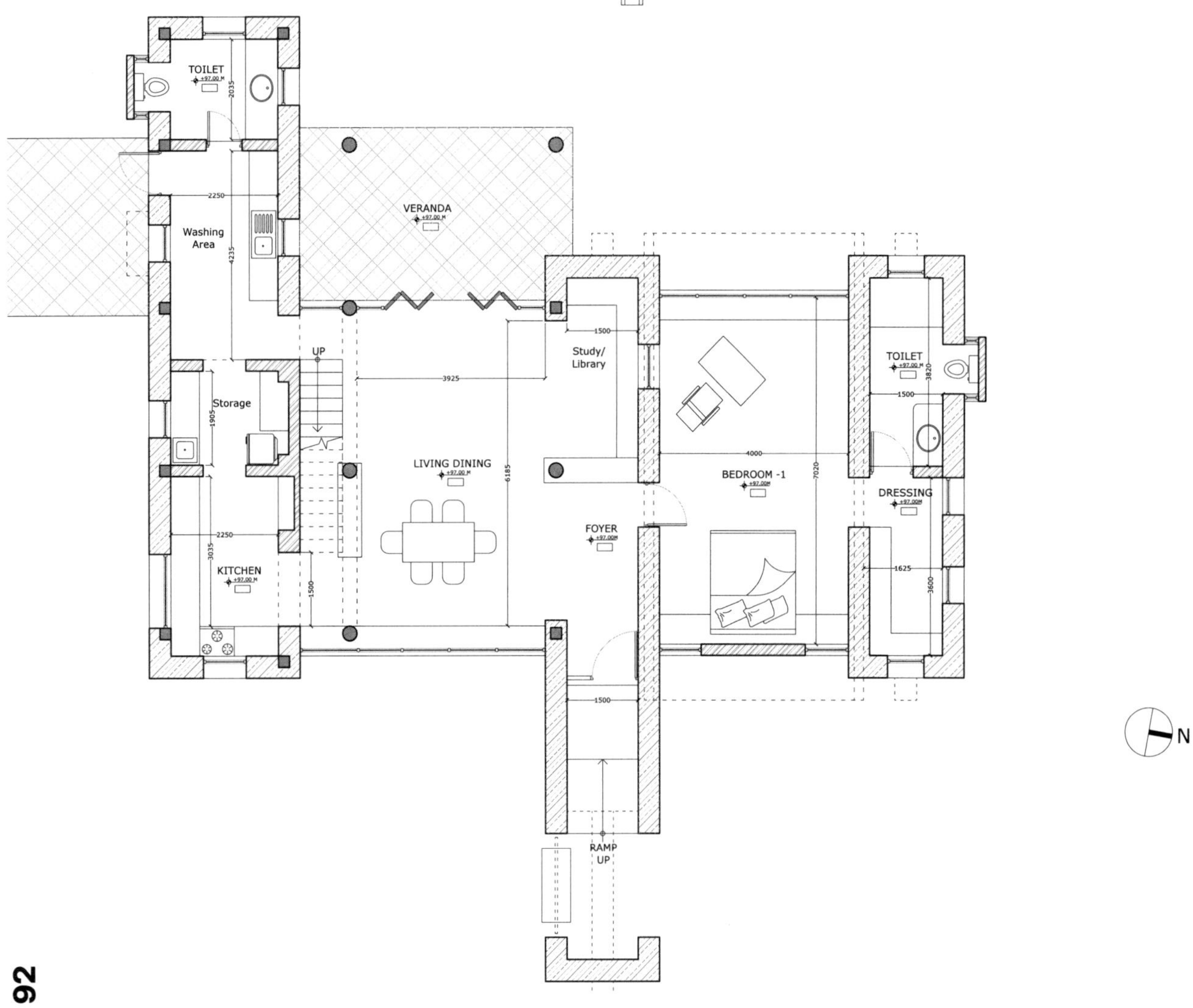
TOILET
2035
2250
VERANDA
Washing Area
4235
UP
1500
Study/ Library
3925
TOILET
3820
1500
Storage
1905
LIVING DINING
6185
4000
BEDROOM -1
7020
DRESSING
FOYER
2250
3035
KITCHEN
1500
1625
3600
1500
RAMP UP
N

HOUSE FOR
KETAN SHAH & FAMILY
HOUSE FOR
ATUL SHAH & FAMILY
Overhead water tank
and wind mill
T.B.M.=100.00
N

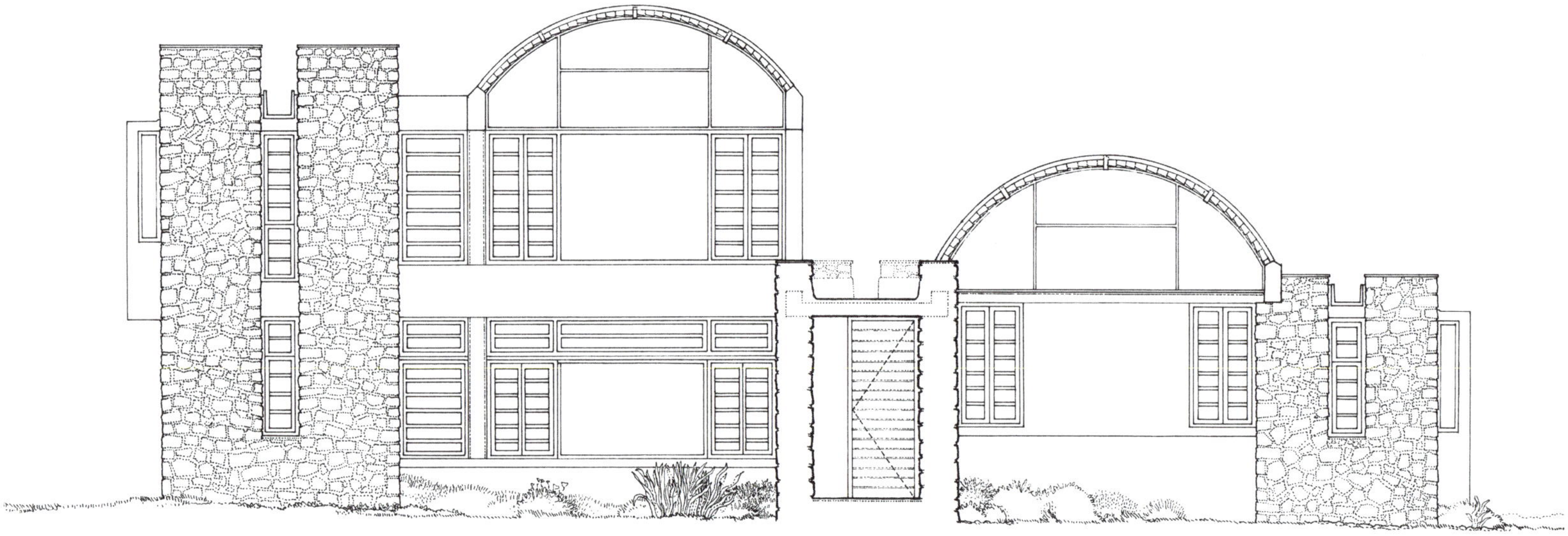

Kaushal

Built at the edge of a river on agricultural land, the complex is shared by two residences for Atul Shah and Ketan Shah, based in Bombay who needed a secondary residence to spend time with their family and perhaps move there permanently and dedicate their time to organic farming and holistic living.

Slow Architecture

Interview with Anupama Kundoo
by Martha Thorne

Martha Thorne: *You have been practicing architecture now for about 25 years. You have always been involved in practice, research, and teaching. Could you speak about your motivations and about how you bring these three areas together?*

Anupama Kundoo: I am glad you have started with this question because for me the whole profession of architecture is about synthesis. It's about bringing various aspects together through design. More specifically to me, it means expanding knowledge continuously. We have to bring spirit and matter together and not only think of technical concerns. We must not forget about what the soul needs, or psychological needs or human scale in additional to functional needs along with climatic needs and many others. This integration is what is embodied in design. For me, it is natural then to try to bring things together. Architecture has to do with developing the capacities to integrate. This reminds me of the words of an engineering professor, who told us that the strength of the chain (technically speaking) lies in its weakest link. So no matter how large or strong those other links are if there is one that is made of thread that will be the strength of the whole chain. So I came to the conclusion early on that if I didn't develop in an integrated way and evolve, then I would have some strong links, but the weakest ones would decide the strength of my entire practice.

I realized that architecture is a process of continuous discovery and understanding of the construct of the world around us. I like to think of a tripod with one foot in each area – practice, research, and teaching – then there is a balanced expression. In terms of teaching, I don't believe it is really even an activity that produces learning. Rather it is the activity that facilitates which makes learning happen. So if I wouldn't continuously learn or if I remained in my comfort zone and rested only on one of the three legs, then I wouldn't be of so much use. Like many four-legged tables in restaurants, you see in any three of them support for the table and it always seems that there is one that is loose because there is one redundant leg. I want to constantly grow and that is the way I feel alive.

Even if there were periods when I was only devoted to my practice, because it was research-oriented, I was able to construct the learning spaces within the practice to teach myself and to teach others. I saw that the younger generation was reaching out to me and I needed to give back. To do this, I needed to have a learning environment for myself. I therefore managed to define three spaces where I can continuously attend to that. I often say that I have a research-oriented practice and practice-oriented teaching. I always try to make my approach holistic.

— *It is often difficult to have a research-oriented practice because it is something that is difficult to make economically viable. Clients are not prone to funding research. How are you able to come to grips with that?*

Around 10 years into my practice, someone commented that my work is all about sustainability, and I was asked if my practice was "sustainable" (economically). My answer was "no." Maybe I am idealistic, but I never thought of my profession as a source of work just to earn money. I feel we almost earn money to be able to work, as it gives meaning to my life. Of course, we all need to subsist, but money alone is not reason enough to make me do things. I also felt that the tasks in India, that I, as an architect, felt that I had to do, were so insurmountable, that nobody would pay for it. Nobody pays for urban design. Nobody would pay for many other things, such as the actual building up of knowledge.

If my concern was more about money, I would probably not even have left Mumbai. I have always done bold and risky things. But again those risks made me feel alive. So even though my office doesn't always sustain itself from jobs, I feel that being able to give that kind of time to my practice helps sustain me in my soul. And I think the money eventually comes around from wherever. When I devote a lot of time to a project, I believe I become more knowledgeable and cleverer because of it and in turn, more employable. Architecture, to really do things well, takes a lot of time. And I think time is my main resource. As a human being time is all I have, and that is one resource I am not willing to waste on things I don't believe in. I like to contradict the notion that "time is money." This, I believe is a mistake that came about after industrialization.

— Please explain about your work in Auroville, India, and how things have changed over time there?

When I first heard of Auroville, I was in the third year of my architecture studies. I used to be very active as a student and participated in a lot of extracurricular activities to complement what I was learning in school. During a summer conference, I came to know that there was a place called Auroville, which was planned as an experimental city. The founder of the city wrote a mission statement that said: Let there be a place on Earth which belongs to no nation as such, but would be there for humanity as a whole. There were radical ideas, such as in the city land could not be owned because all the problems began with ownership of things. Not possessing things is liberating. At the time, I was living in Mumbai. It was not very common at that time for a young woman to be living on her own, renting an apartment, while having parents who were living nearby. I was very self-reliant and independent and when I couldn't afford my Mumbai bills and to live in the areas I liked without being a wage slave, I decided to move. I was thinking of continuing my studies abroad, but instead of going to the US, I thought it best to stay in India where my family was and not rush from one school to another. I thought it would be good to learn more about rural India. I was really very naïve and set off with a backpack, which was also not common, and I decided to go to this radical place called Auroville, where I knew some people, perhaps staying for a week or so. I liked the sense of adventure and freedom so much that I just stayed on. When I was there, I had limited means. I lived there for 15 years, of which the first nearly 10 were spent in a thatch hut, using my bicycle, motor bike and solar panels for all electricity. This was probably a blessing because you have to be ingenious when you don't have a lot of resources.

Now when I look back, I think what I really liked about Auroville was that it was radically visionary. And despite everything that was difficult, it carried on. It was not envisioned to be a commune, it was planned as a collective experiment towards an ideal city involving all the nations, living together. It is an example of a holistic rethinking of everything from education to economy. My personal approach is that, instead of whining and complaining about problems, I prefer to work on a new solution directly, to be creative. I found that Auroville could be very fertile ground for me to explore solutions, instead of just complaining about the way things were. So I went there with an open mind.

Of course, there are problems in Auroville even today. There was an incredible vision for a future city even though the urban aspect actually hasn't taken off. As in many grand projects, it meets with human resistance, from inside, too. Projects like this mean that people have to change. There are many short-comings. I can draw a parallel with a book, *Animal Farm* by George Orwell, and all the problems that arose in that community.

I still work towards the realization of Auroville in whichever way I can, even though I don't live there. The Human Resources Development Ministry of India has taken this project under its wing to facilitate this ambitious international experiment. I feel that the conditions for this "future city lab" have been enabled. There is a place for this type of initiative.

A few years after moving to Auroville, I met Roger Anger, the chief architect of Auroville, who had built extensively in Paris, and whose monograph *Research on Beauty: Architecture 1953-2008,* I later authored. I believe Auroville was misunderstood. People assumed it was to be like a Brasilia, and India already had Chandigarh – with formal-looking new city plans. I think Roger Anger's master plan for Auroville was also misunderstood in the light of other events at the time. In reality, he was rethinking modernism without motorism, and that changes everything. It brings another type of mobility and street quality, as in Venice. For me, it is still one of the highest visions I have seen. I believe in the collective evolution of our profession. I don't mind working on other architect's projects after they have passed away. I think it is a project worthy of further work and it is a great opportunity for India.

— Please talk a little about craft and traditional building methods. It seems that in the West, we have handicraft, which is at one end of the spectrum, and technology, almost divorced from the human hand, at the other. I have a feeling that perhaps in India, because of its history, culture, population, economics, there seems to be more of an integration of different techniques across the spectrum.

I am very excited by the future and in general, I am not nostalgic about tradition. I am more excited by the future. I would rather take references from the future that we can imagine rather than from the past. Having said that, personally, I have always been involved in making things with my hands – food, knitting, painting ... I have found it both empowering and joyful. The hand is an integrating element, it is not just connected with the brain. Let me give you an example, in India, we sit on the floor and eat with our hands. Children are only taught later to use a knife and fork. Our hands are versatile, and spontaneously they can work as a spoon or a fork according to the need. The hands are somehow intelligent.

My family was uprooted from Bengal after the partition and I grew up in Mumbai, so I don't feel nostalgic about the past. Sometimes being attached to the past is like carrying baggage and that is the part of craft that I don't like. There is a habitual past. Even though the problem is new, out of habit people continue to make the same things in the same way.

In rural India, I was able to see that people who were not industrialized were able to solve their problems – they were very "hands-on". This was fascinating. This was not so much about crafts they made, more about the ingenuity that humans have developed. It is more an appreciation of the hands to think rather than let the hands just go on replicating something from the past.

When I moved to a small place, I realized that it was the industrial revolution that divided this world into two camps. We needed to design the tools that would then produce things. Those who did the thinking devised the tools for the others to then produce things. This was when people became alienated from meeting their own needs. I also realized that many places undergoing rapid urbanization, like India, had not gone through mainstream industrialization and were having solutions imposed upon them that were causing more problems than they were solving. So, I said, "We are not industrialized, so let's not think as if we are. What can we do here that makes sense?" When I started including craftspeople in the work, it was purely out of rational and often engineering reasons. Even though something may look similar to a traditional craft, it was a critical re-thinking of material choices and the skills. It is not so-called "vernacular", because it is not how people traditionally built in my area. It was introduced. Of course, I have also learned from conventional methods and have implemented them, too.

I like the sentence of Charles and Ray Eames (American designers, ed.) that says something like innovation is not there for its own sake. It is only necessary if we have identified genuine problems that design could solve. So that is the way I proceeded.

— *When you are faced with a new project or commission, how do you start? What is the process you follow?*

First and foremost, I try to figure out what the building is for, not the typology such as hotel or house. I try to understand and to always remember that architecture has to support the nature of the life that will take place in it and only be a backdrop. So I try to find out what the life is that is supposed to occur there. I spend a lot of time understanding the physical and spatial requirements, but not neglecting the psychological needs of the person. Meanwhile, I do parallel research that starts with the place and the understanding of the available materials, skills and livelihoods of the people in that place.

I have created my own formula or my own strategy for approaching a new project. There are two things I look at: the users or those who are going to occupy the voids that I am going to design; and then a whole lot of other people, who are going to be involved through the making of the architecture. By a lot, I don't just limit this to the masons or those who work on site, for example, but also include the people who are involved in the all related building industries, from procuring building material to the making of sophisticated infrastructural materials. On one hand, there is the life that will take place, and on the other hand, there are livelihoods that are associated with the making of the building. This involves the socioeconomic impact of the building, including what kind of skills we should be promoting, how the money can remain in the local economy, etc. So I try to apply a holistic vision. I design the material part of the architecture as well as the non-material part as a cohesive whole. In an appropriate way, I try to balance design decisions keeping in mind the life of the users with the livelihoods of the people of the place. That is the way I begin.

— *Your exhibition at the Louisiana has the subtitle* Taking Time. *Why did you choose this subtitle? What is the importance or meaning of time in architecture?*

There are many, many layers of meaning for me in that combination of words. The first one is that I feel that you cannot *make* time. People are always saying that they need to make time for this or that. We are living beings and we cannot make time, we can only *take* time. I prefer to be proactive. You are born with

Martha Thorne is an American architectural academic, curator and author. She is the Executive Director of the Pritzker Architecture Prize and Dean of IE School of Architecture and Design, Madrid/Segovia, Spain.

your time, so spend it well. For me, to take time is to be alive. Now that I am getting older I feel that the best thing that I have learned is to prioritize the expenditure of that precious resource – time – for the right thing.

When I graduated from architecture school, a lot of people in my generation were worried about settling into the right jobs, trying to make ends meet. Young people tried to plan what they would earn and how they would spend it or save it, and what they would do in the future. This all felt like fiction to me, because passion, self-development and service to society did not necessarily feature. I wondered why they didn't mind doing a job eight hours a day that they didn't like, being a wage slave, not contributing anything to society because they were not inspired, just to get some money to pay, for example, for a bad apartment. I felt people were unconsciously ready to sacrifice their deeper fulfilment and being true to their sense of purpose. For me it was important to remain true to myself and be driven by my aspiration, individually as well as collectively. If we do things for each other in a community, it doesn't cost anything but leads to enrichment for all.

Now as we focus on sustainability, I have tried to find the central issue of where we went wrong and why we are in such a predicament. I think a place we may have gone wrong is when we started believing that time is money. We made a lot of wrong time-saving decisions to save money. We often thought that it was better to buy something instead of making it ourselves. But this was wrong. Time is life, time is not money. Time is living. If you spend your time well, you are happy. You don't have the urge to go shopping to flee, you are more relaxed and less stressed. You can become more in tune with your body and feel better.

I am so interested in long-term thinking rather than short-term actions. In India, we seem to have an urgency to act in construction. All over the world, we seem to do things with such urgency. I have realized all the more that what we really need is time to think. We cannot cut corners. We need to take time to think first before we act. If people just go ahead and take action it's almost always wrong. And what's more, people are not even taking the time to reflect on incorrect actions and that creates wrong habits. So I would like to take time and have us create the right habits, which will serve us. And for that, we need to take time.

By being peacefully connected to yourself, you can produce a lot of things. I would urge people to go for 'slow architecture', where you don't cut corners on thinking. Take time to build knowledge and to build community. In the end, it's like the hare and the tortoise and slow but steady you will win the race. If you did the right thing, everything you did would be useful for the next project.

One final message I would like to give to younger generations as well, is that I feel that architecture didn't start with me. My work did not start when I was born nor will it end when I die. We are part of a large collective action in time and in space. As a human society, we are building this knowledge collectively. It is a process of evolution and we have to realize where we stand within the whole thing. It doesn't start with us. I want to put time into perspective. I have been in practice for 30 years. It has been very rewarding and I feel very rich as a person. If you see it holistically, I am very happy where I am and to feel alive throughout the day.

Anupama Kundoo was interviewed in January 2020

Multipurpose Hall S.A.W.C.H.U., Auroville, India

Set in the campus of the Indian Pavilion, the Sri Aurobindo World Centre for Human Unity was envisaged as a multipurpose gathering place for the residents of Auroville. The distinctive feature of this building is the lack of walls or doors into the large circular hall. Supported on eight leaning pillars like the many trunks of the banyan tree, the circular hall with its 16 metres in diameter does not have a central trunk; instead the roof slab has a central skylight allowing natural daylight to enter. Apart from two rooms at its rear, there are no walls dividing the inside from the outside. Extending outwards from the central hall in three of the four quadrants, there are tiers of seats, forming a low-rise amphitheatre. The floor slab is integrated into the landscaped treatment of the sloping site so that the transition spaces for informal seating arrive at the ground level of the surrounding grove of trees. Water bodies surround the hall maintaining the calm and quiet ambience of the building. The waterspouts of the roof slab deliver the natural water to the water body on four sides. Geometrically, the circular shape of the hall emphasizes unity. The amphitheatre steps ripple outward and tend to change its shape from circular to square. The last step is a square with rounded corners to imply that the ripples may extend even beyond the physical centre of unity. Exposed reinforced concrete is the principle material. The final volume became 75 cubic metres instead of 125 cubic metres thanks to efficient structural design, circular geometry, with the columns sloping to reduce the roof span significantly, and lost shuttering of ferrocement to cast the radial beams with a non-orthogonal profile. Corners of slabs are reinforced using diagonal steel bars for stiffening, thus shifting the point of support inside to reduce the span without increasing the effective depth and the corresponding volume of concrete.

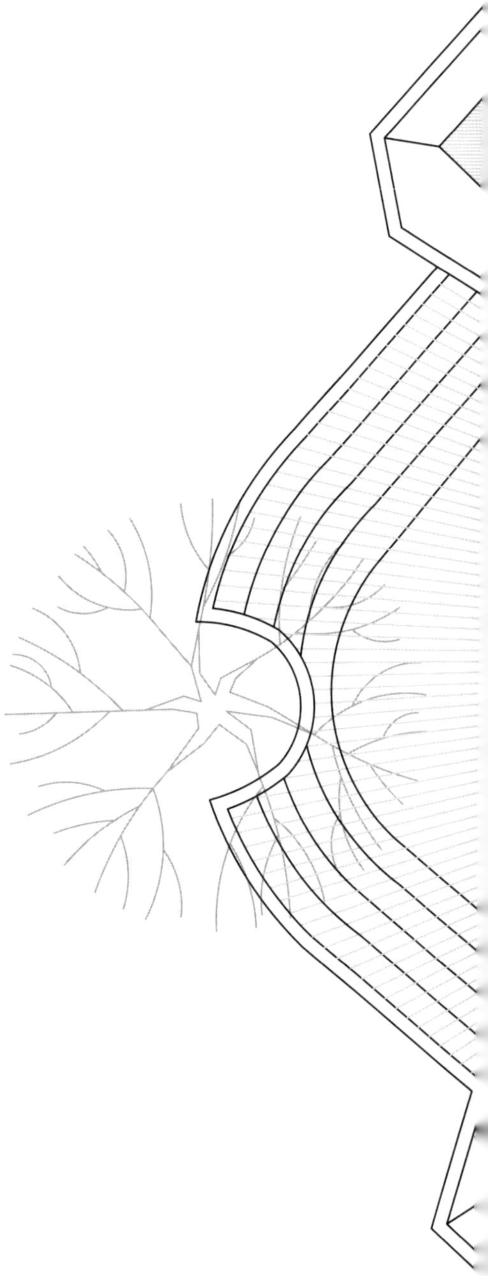

Multipurpose Hall S.A.W.C.H.U., 2000
Auroville, India
307 m²

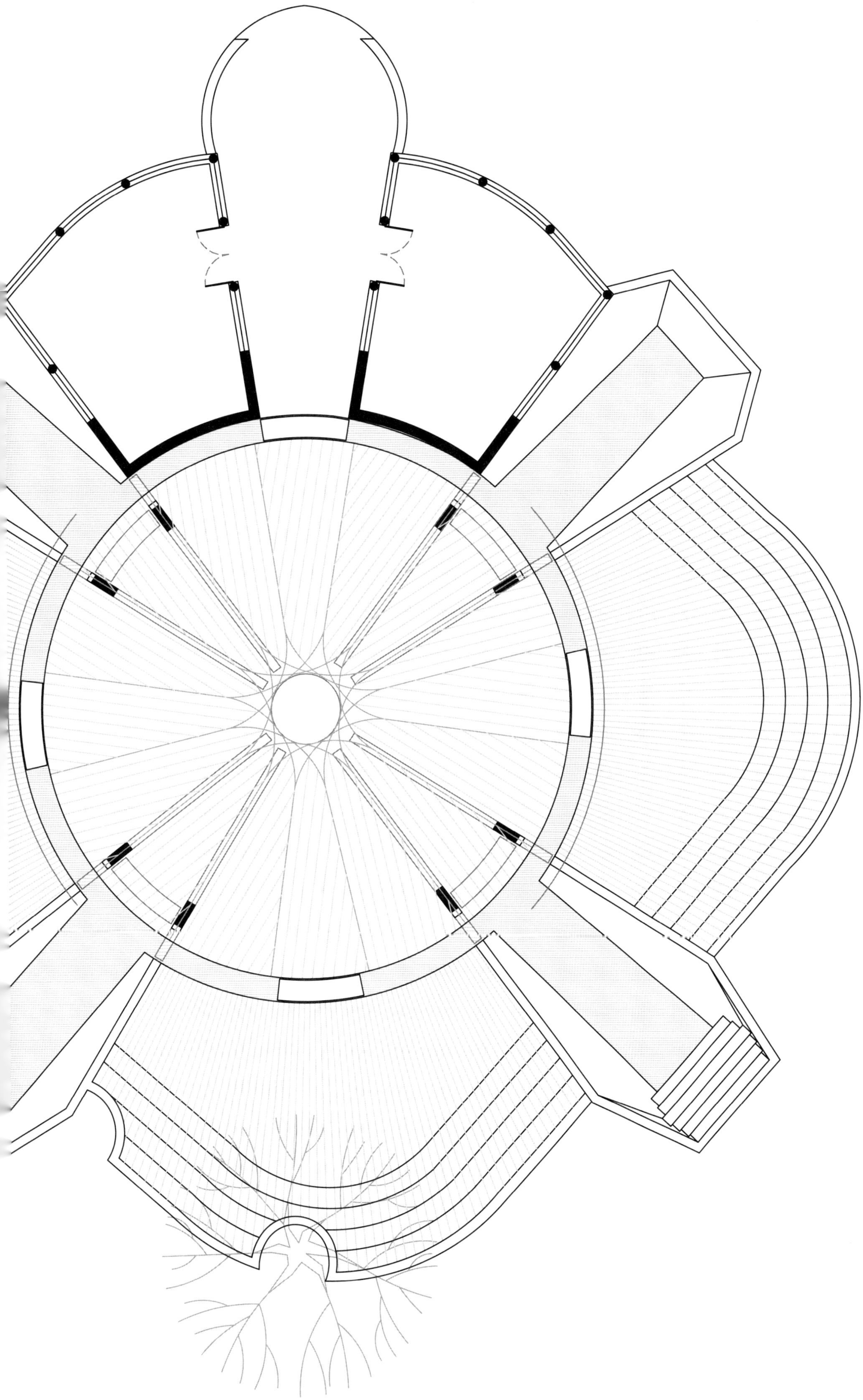

The shape of the radial beams supporting the slab is based on design efficiency, very judiciously using only a minimum of concrete. The shape also adds to the aesthetic quality by softening harsh edges. The efficient shape is enabled by using ferrocement as lost shuttering.

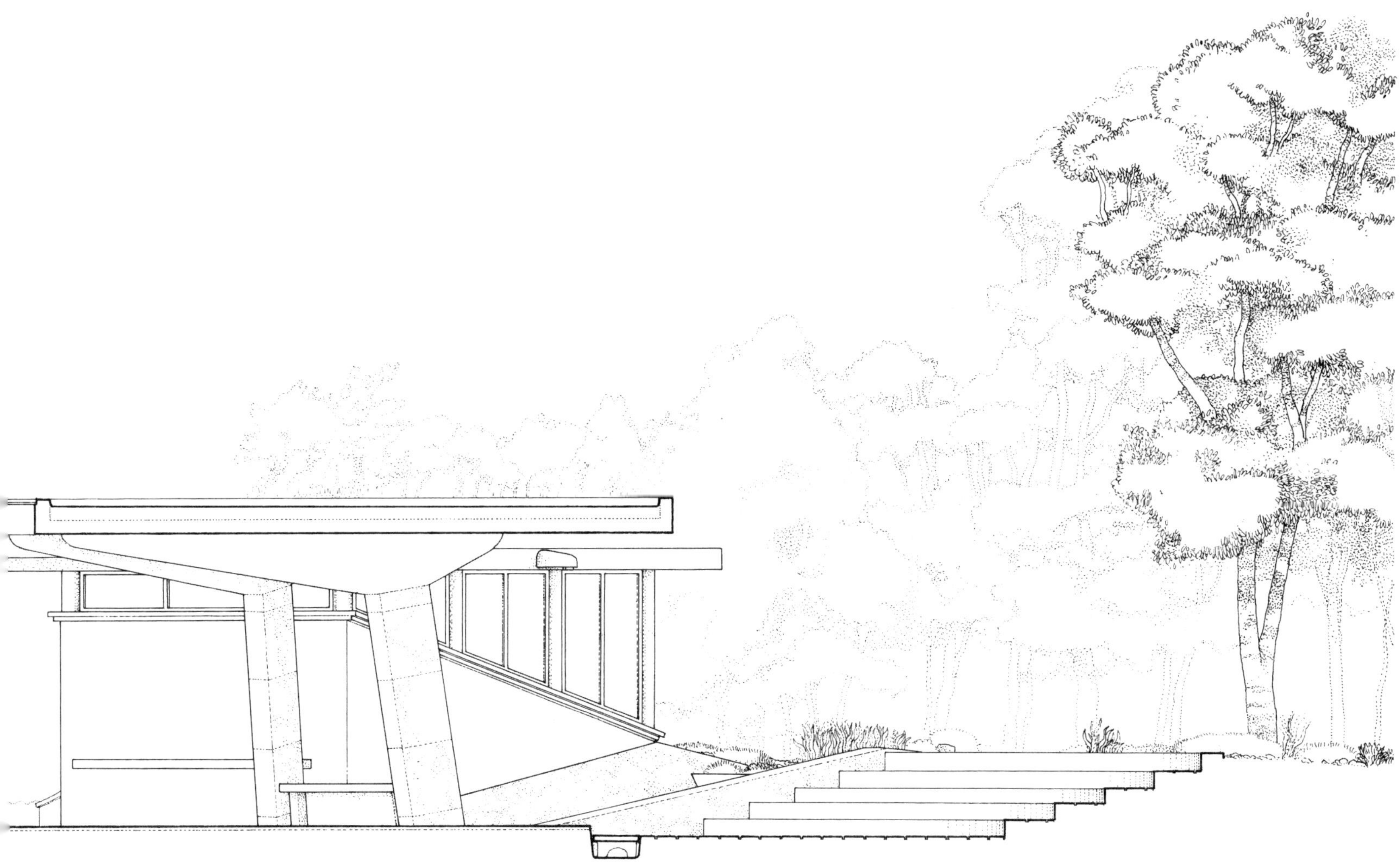

Creativity – An Urban Eco Community, Auroville, India

Inspired by the concept of co-housing, Creativity was planned as a prototype for low-density urban collective living with the focus on affordability and a positive environmental impact. The central idea was based on promoting community and sharing, using one of five housing clusters, each accommodating around 50-60 deliberately diverse residents. Different apartment types for singles, couples, families and youth groups are arranged around a central courtyard. Residents share common facilities such as kitchen, laundry and guest facilities at the cluster level, and a multipurpose hall and gallery at the neighbourhood level. The aim was to find a balance between each resident's need for individual space as well as for contact with the collectivity. Streets are created on the upper levels to facilitate communication, and these are constructed as detached walkways not touching the facade, so as to give the homes the necessary privacy. The voids thus created between the building and the bridge-like streets on the two upper levels also promote natural ventilation through the increase in the air stack as per the Venturi effect. This strategy, alongside insulated roofs and cross ventilation, allows maximum climatic comfort. The excavated onsite soil was used to build rammed earth walls in a technique using an especially large body of formwork, adding five per cent cement for water resistance, and lending a contemporary character to a material associated with the vernacular. Specially designed trapezoidal terracotta roofing units laid on part-prefab beams were designed to achieve rapid modular construction of roofing slabs with high insulation properties. Terracotta pots as lost shuttering in filler slab technology were used to span the multipurpose and dining halls to economise on structural steel and eliminate the need for plastering or painting. A root-zone treatment plant recycles treated sewage water for irrigation.

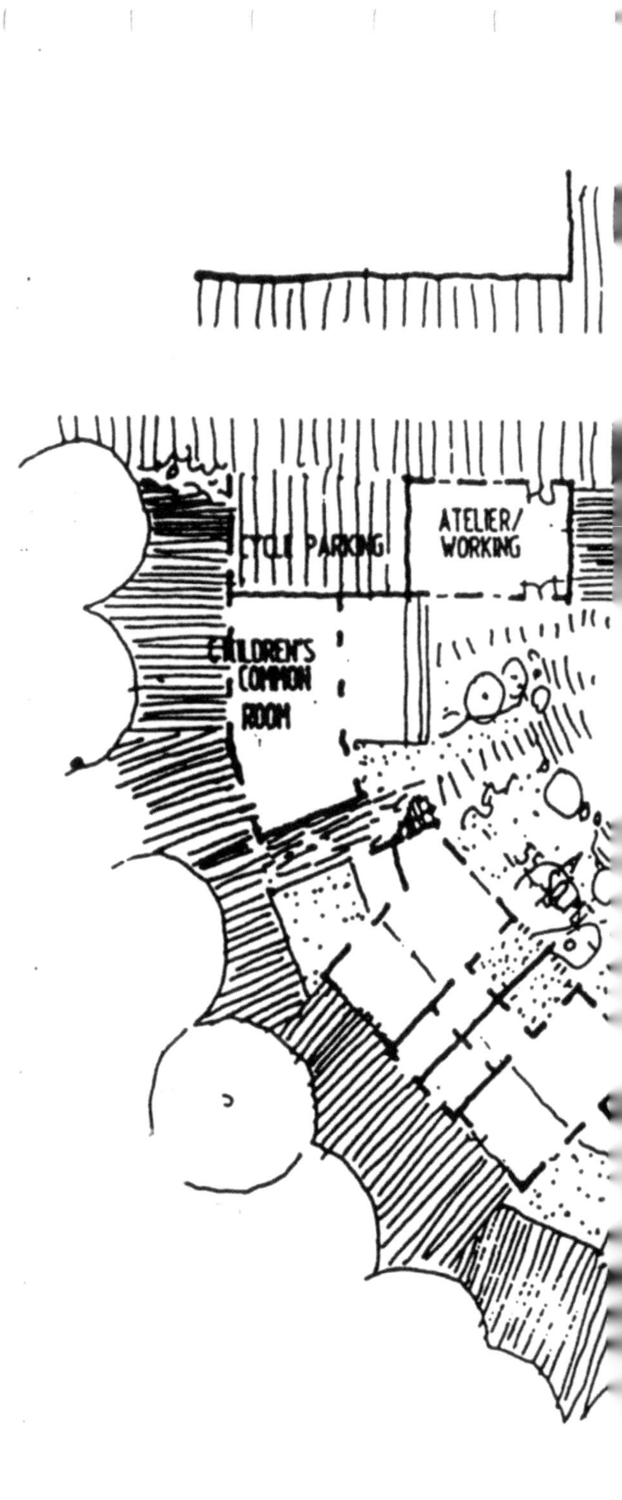

Creativity – An Urban Eco Community, 2003
Auroville, India
3,252 m^2

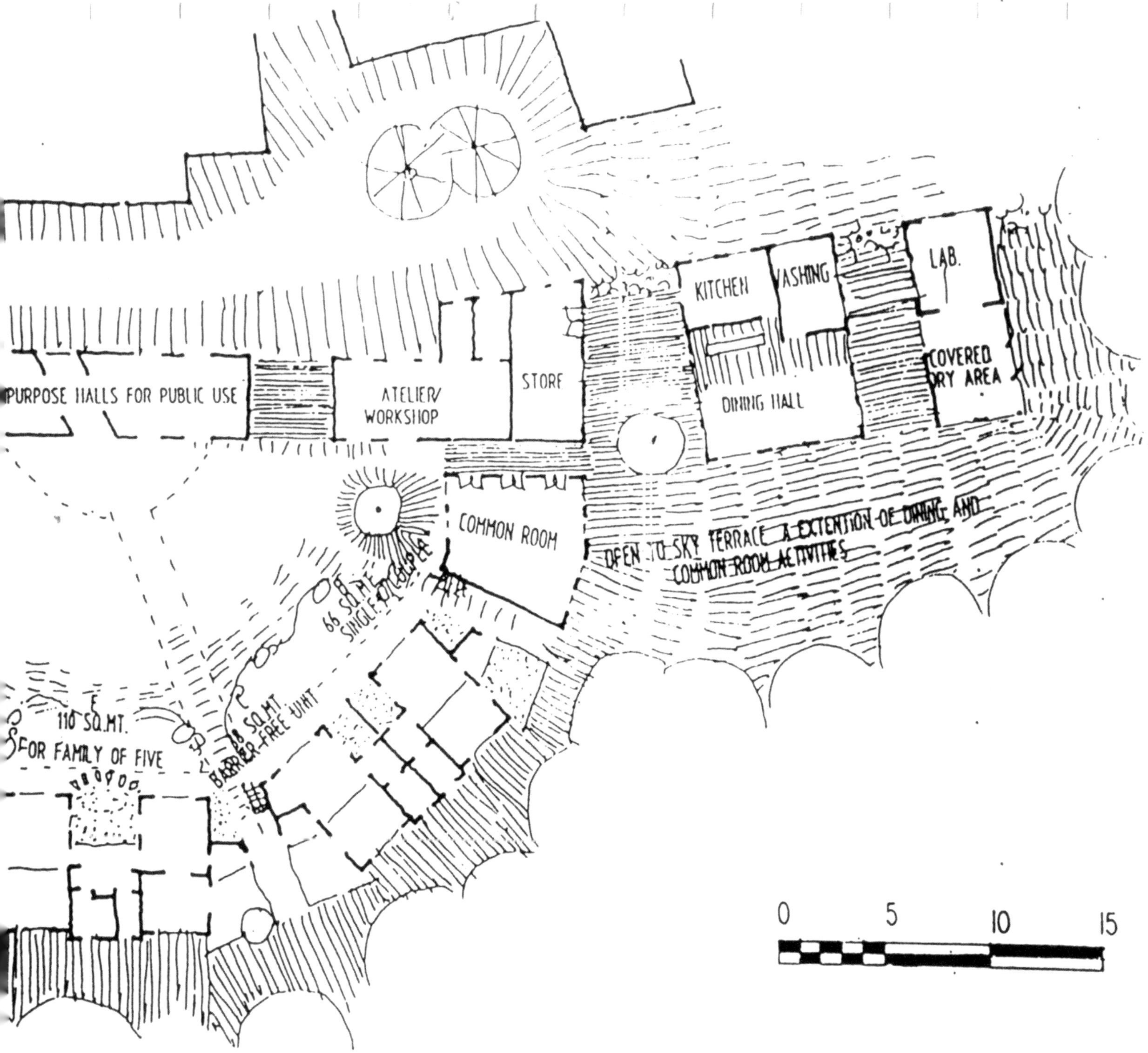
PURPOSE HALLS FOR PUBLIC USE
ATELIER/ WORKSHOP
STORE
KITCHEN
WASHING
LAB.
COVERED
RY AREA
DINING HALL
COMMON ROOM
OPEN TO SKY TERRACE A EXTENTION OF DINING AND COMMON ROOM ACTIVITIES
66 SQ.MT. SINGLE COUPLE
110 SQ.MT. FOR FAMILY OF FIVE
88 SQ.MT. BARRIER FREE UNIT
0
5
10
15

BED ROOM
TER.
DINING
BED ROOM
DINING
LIVING
VER
COURTYARD

‘Streets’ on upper levels facilitate community life but are detached from the building to enhance natural ventilation and the required privacy. A large insulated roof projects like an umbrella with the monsoon in mind.

Hollow trapezoid terracotta units, handmade on site, provide insulated roofs in a 'jack-arch-like' system with its assembly supported by slim, partly prefabricated concrete beams.

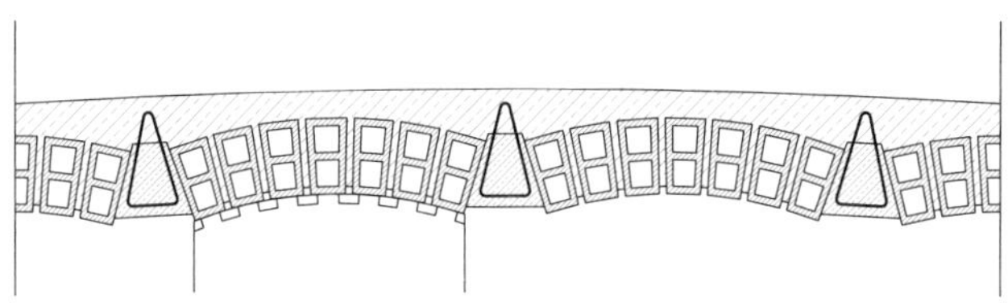

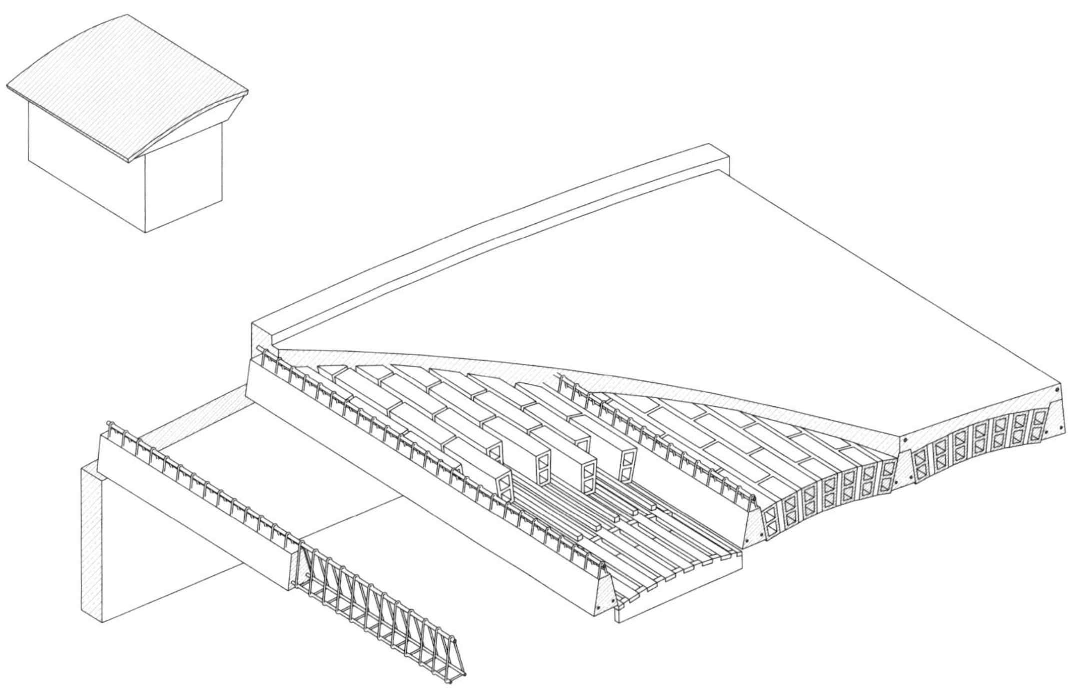

Traditional terracotta cooking pots are used inverted as lost shuttering formwork for a concrete filler slab, enabling savings on steel.

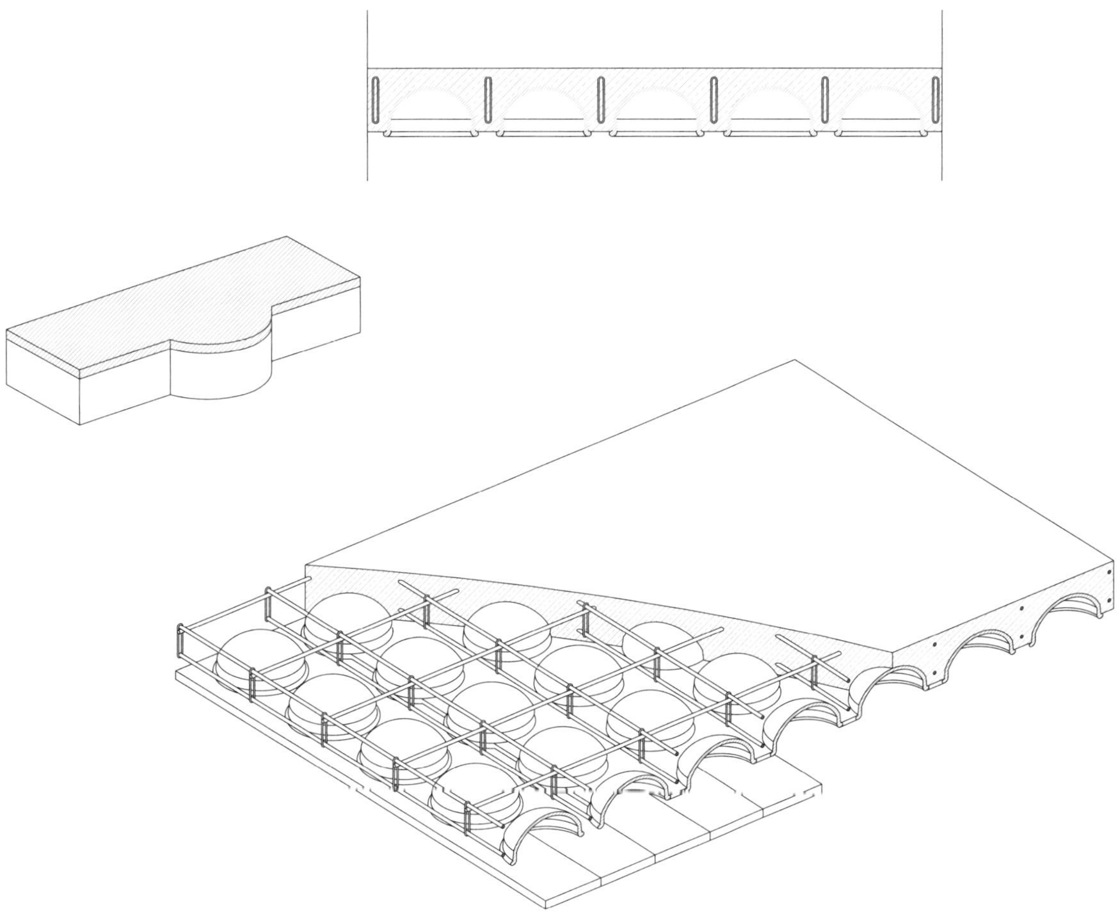

Terracotta units used in jack-arch or filler slab systems permit roofing solutions that are speedy to construct, and reduce steel consumption and therefore costs significantly. Moreover, this supports the local economy by including locally produced materials and employing local labour.

Mitra Youth Hostel, Auroville, India

Mitra Youth Hostel is a facility designed to welcome visiting youth for short- and medium-term stays in Auroville. Located in the planned city centre of Auroville, and based on the architect's urban design for the area, this three-storey building is situated in the habitat belt of the city's central administrative area very close to the Town Hall Complex also designed by Anupama Kundoo. With single and double rooms, and two dormitories per floor, a total of 60 people can be accommodated during full occupancy. The design arranges the various rooms along a singly loaded corridor, which bends along the assigned plot in an obtuse angle that encloses a paved courtyard that is shaded by the building and therefore usable by the residents as a public space. Terraces and spaces for occupation by smaller groups on various floor levels allow the hostel to have a social nature facilitating contact among residents. Each room has a small private balcony. Common bathrooms and kitchens are provided for each floor as spaces that foster sharing and community living while also making the facility affordable for visiting youth from diverse backgrounds. An external staircase allows people to return to their rooms without having to enter by way of an office or administration desk. The building is constructed with plastered brick masonry and reinforced-concrete slabs.

Mitra Youth Hostel, 2005
Auroville, India
1,114 m^2

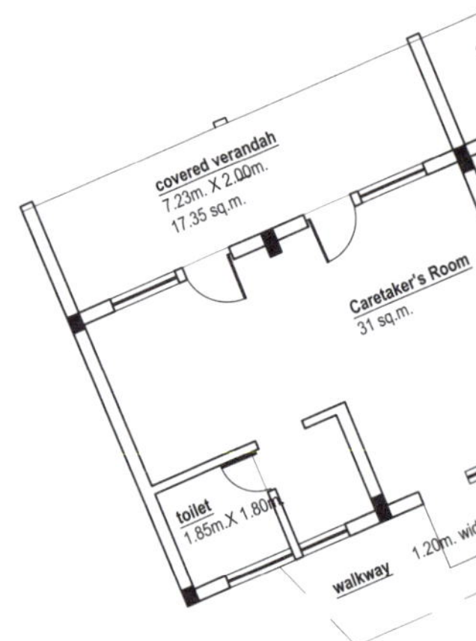
covered verandah
7.23m. X 2.00m.
17.35 sq.m.
Caretaker's Room
31 sq.m.
toilet
walkway

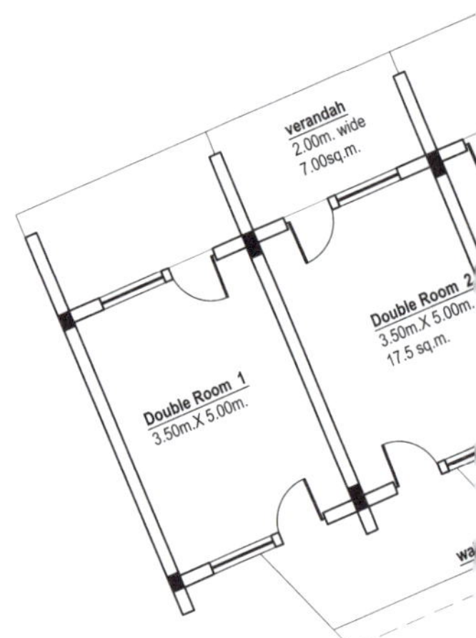
verandah
2.00m. wide
7.00sq.m.
Double Room 1
3.50m.X 5.00m.
Double Room 2
3.50m.X 5.00m.
17.5 sq.m.

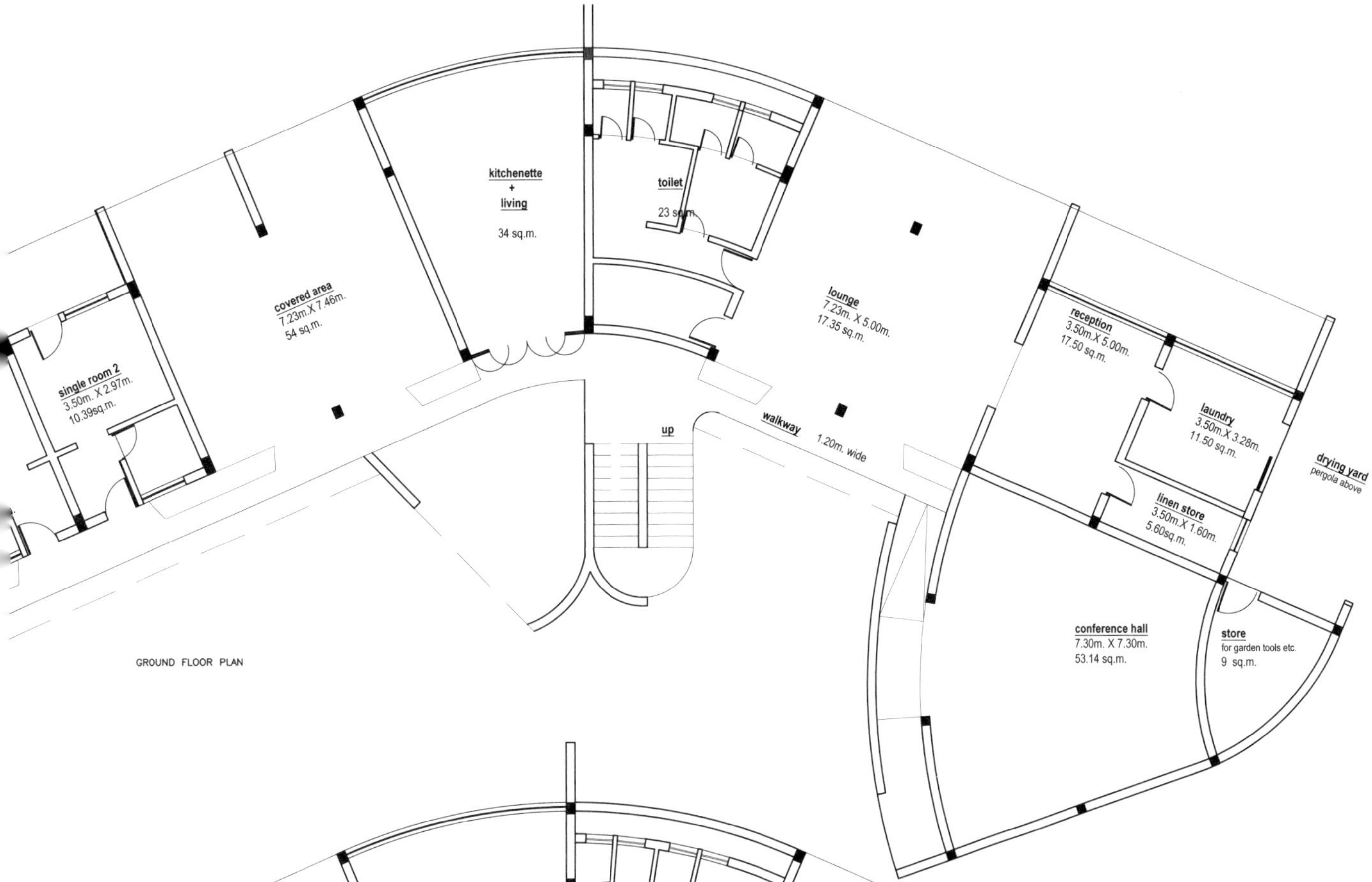

GROUND FLOOR PLAN

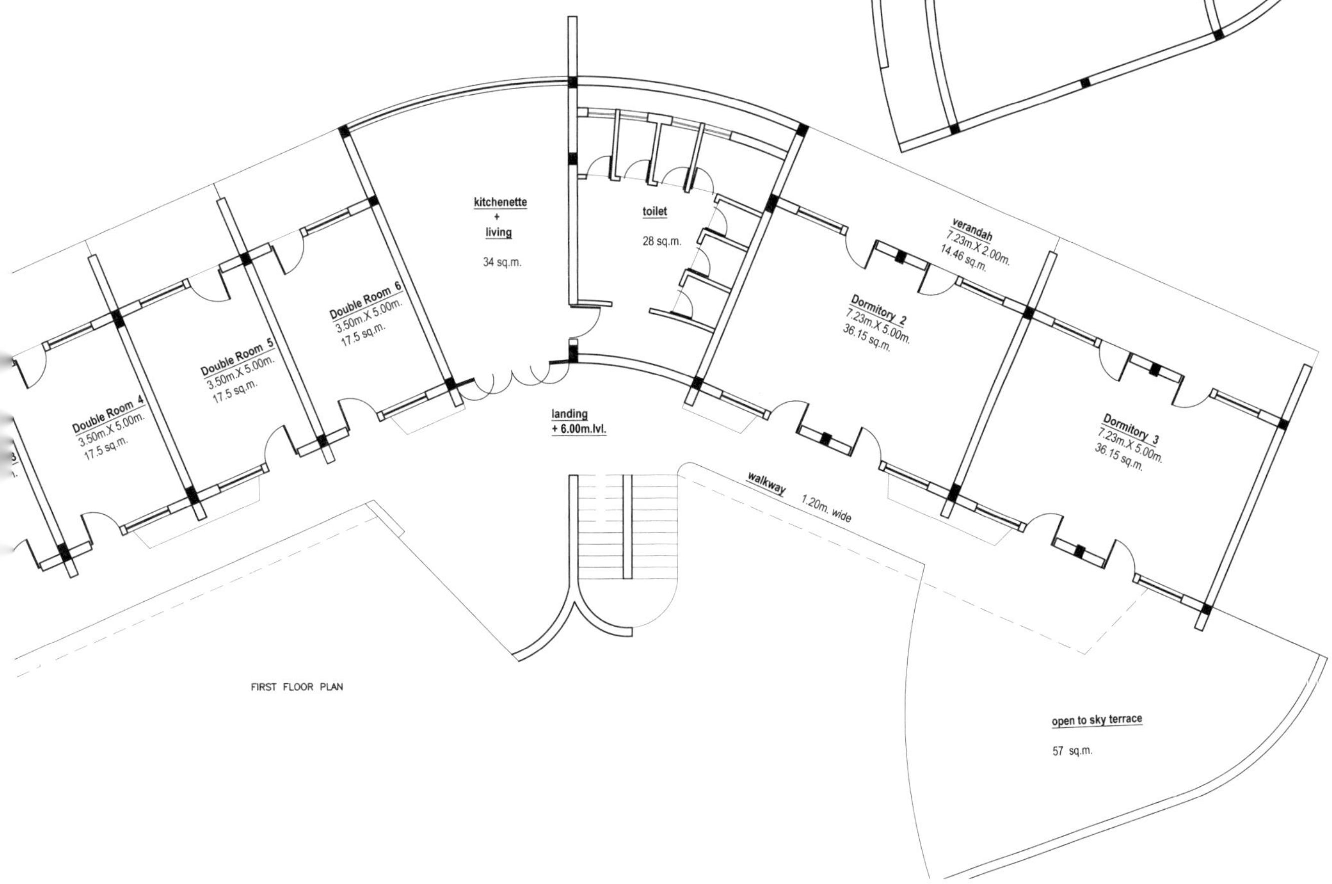

FIRST FLOOR PLAN

Town Hall Complex, Auroville, India

The growing administrative needs of Auroville made it too small to build the main Town Hall as envisaged by the chief architect, Roger Anger, so the current requirements were accommodated in smaller buildings called Town Hall Annex. Such a move was meant to ensure that these buildings would herald the realisation of the future city and the 'real' Town Hall. The challenge was how to create an urban feeling with only the three buildings that the programme involved: the Auroville Centre for Urban Research, including offices for the working committee, housing and land management, as well as Auroville's planning; a multimedia centre; and a cafeteria and related social infrastructure. The aim was to define the language of the interconnecting elements such that the buildings would have a compact, urban character. The offices were thus interspersed with service and public circulation areas. The central public space between the two buildings overlooking the cafeteria is the heart of the complex. Walkways, bridges and ramps provide shaded links between buildings. The buildings are mainly constructed in reinforced concrete and brick masonry to establish a sense of permanence and stability suited to the programme. Various elements demonstrate the material's capacity for large-span roofs and cantilevers, as a celebration of engineering achievements: the large overhangs containing the walkways along the future lake promenade, the large cantilever over the cafeteria roof supported by only two pillars, and various ramps and bridges also built as long cantilevers. The complex also includes green infrastructure technologies with 100 per cent of the waste water from toilets being treated and re-used. Roof water is harvested and treated to drinking standards and supplied in the cafeteria. Spaces are planned for adequate daytime lighting through the central skylight using room sizing.

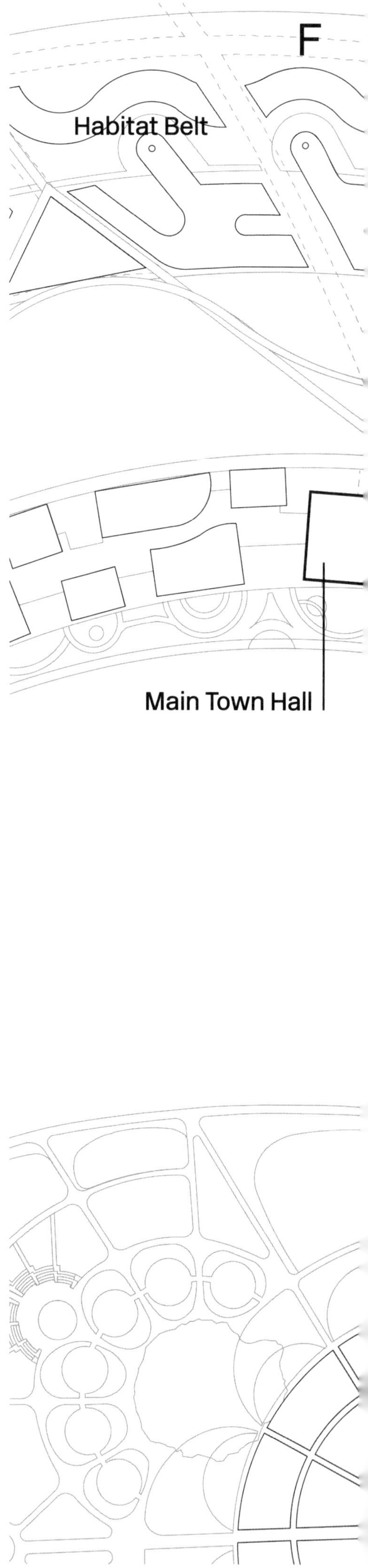

Auroville Town Hall Complex, 2005
Auroville, India
1,703 m^2

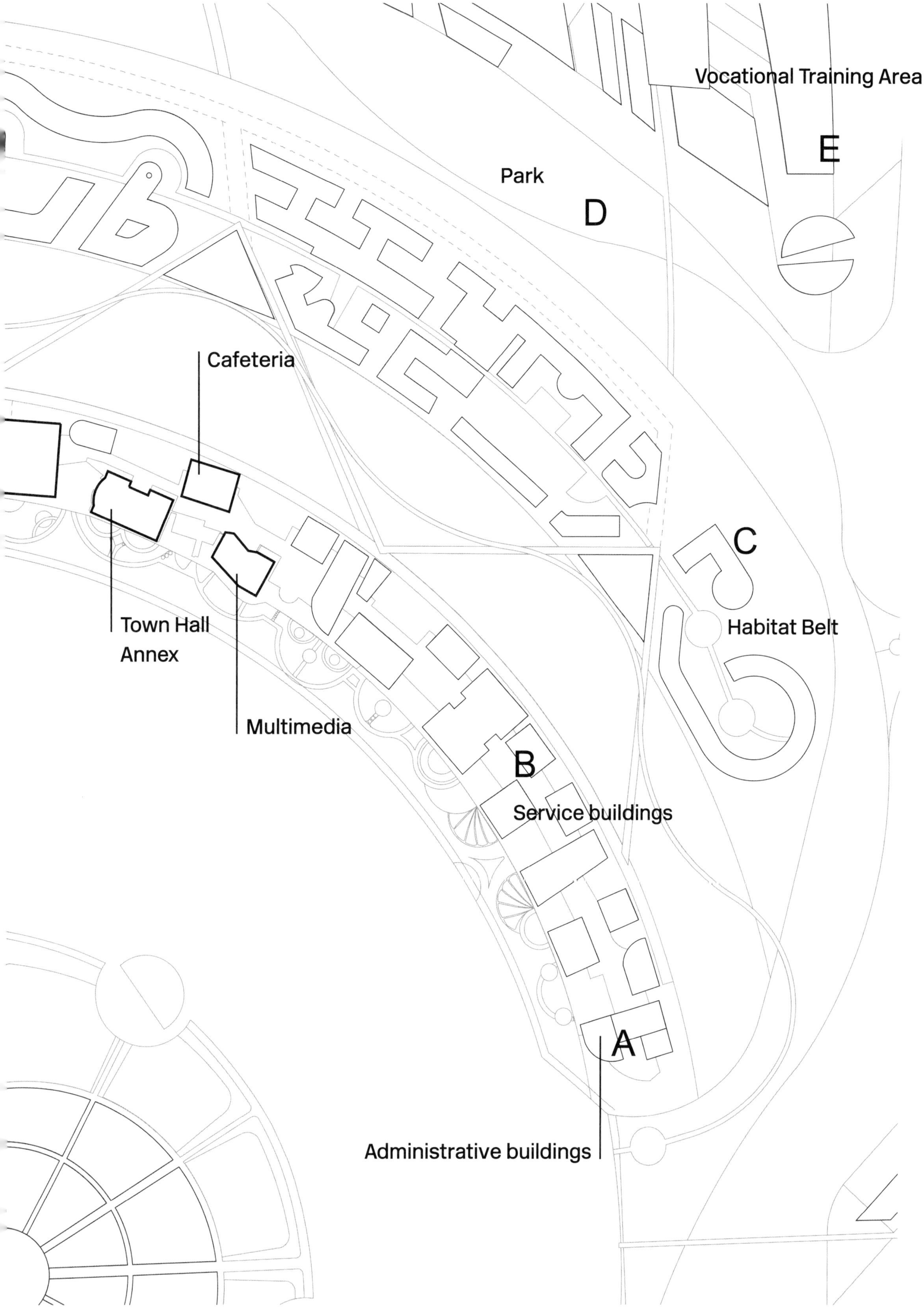
Vocational Training Area
E
Park
D
Cafeteria
C
Habitat Belt
Town Hall
Annex
Multimedia
B
Service buildings
A
Administrative buildings

Kundoo had asked Roger Anger to design the railings of the central atrium and the main staircase, as well as the information counter in the lobby. And he obliged.

Sculpture designed by French artist Chantal Gowa, based in Auroville.

Main Town Hall designed by Kundoo based on Roger Anger's masterplan, as yet unbuilt.

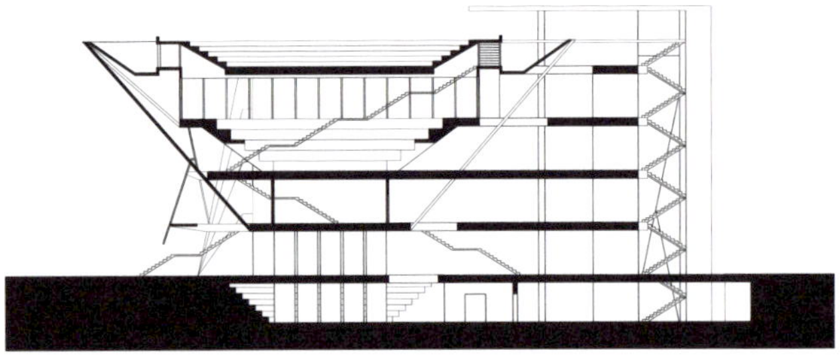

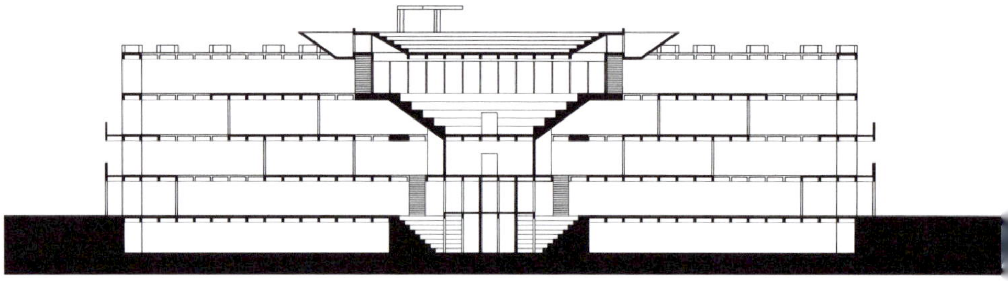

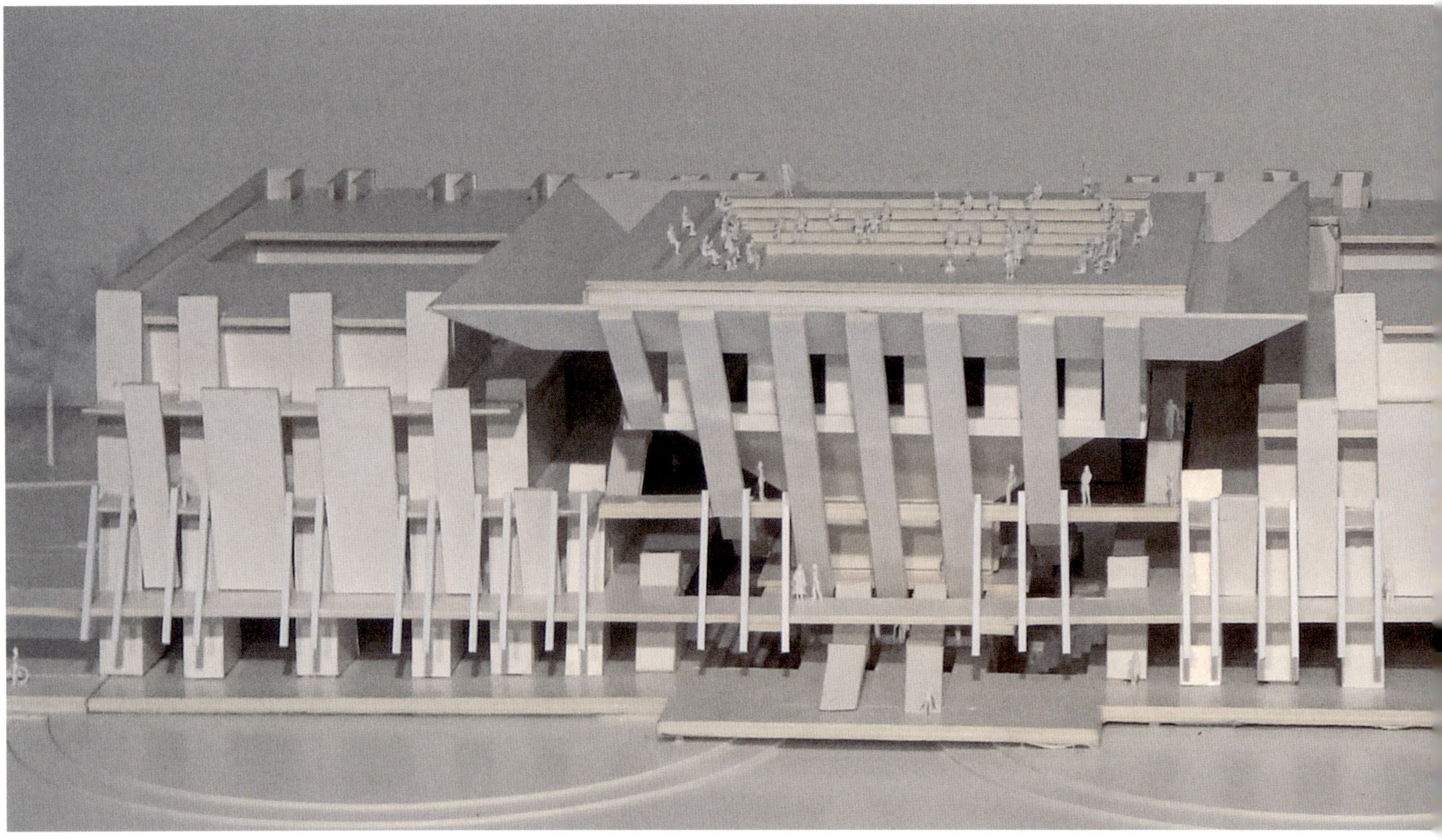

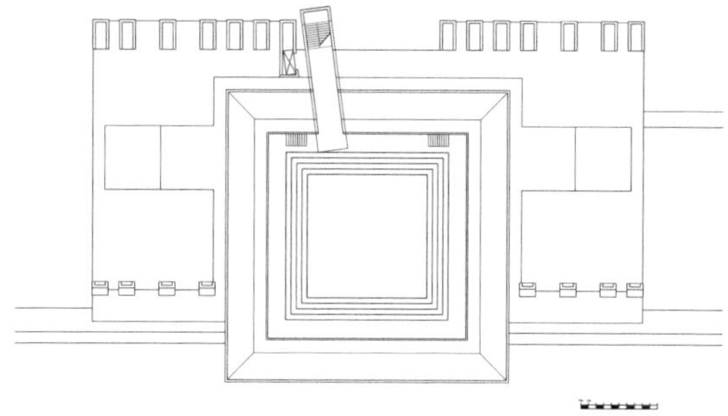

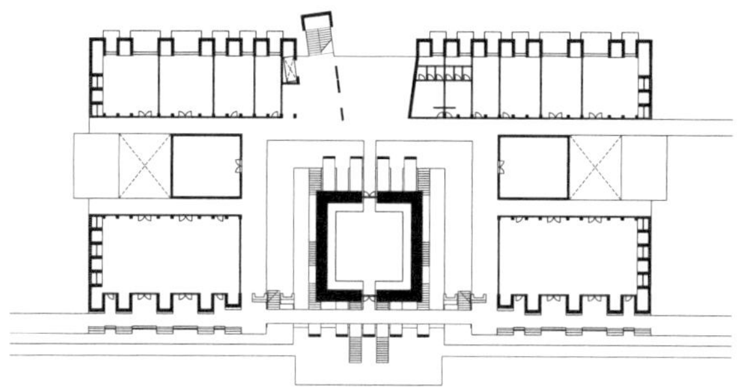

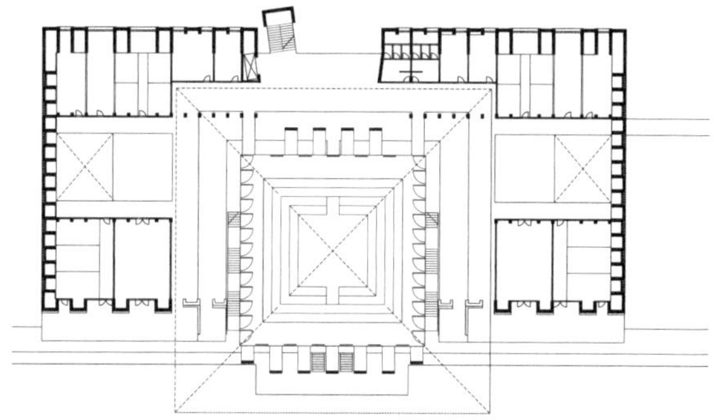

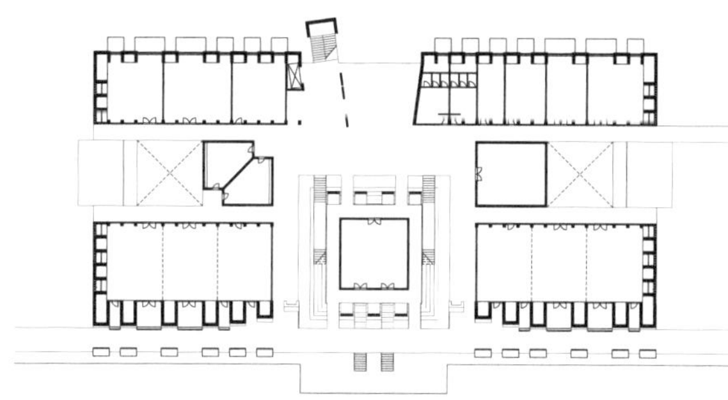

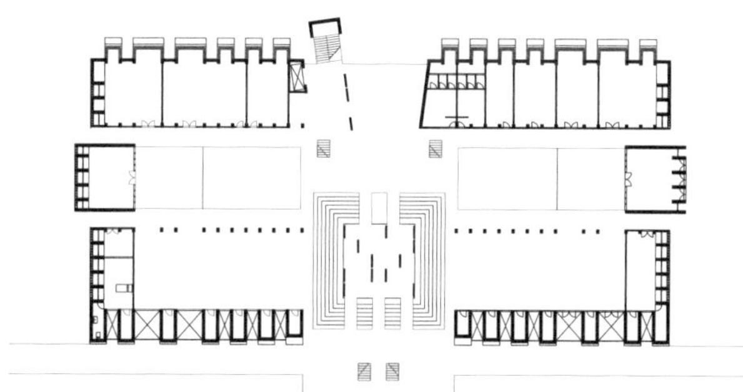

Taking Time

By Anupama Kundoo

Architecture takes time. Not only do **buildings outlive humans,** iconic architecture and cities **take lifetimes to create** over generations. The built environment meanwhile continues to evolve over time corresponding to the evolution of human society. Architecture must **stand the test of time** to be relevant, grounded in long term thinking, built upon past constructs, taking action in the present with a vision of the future and the future of human society in mind. We can prolong the life of our predecessors by working on visions that are still relevant rather than reinventing the wheel and starting with our own ideas each time, as if architecture begins with a clean slate. As contemporary architects are we ready to work on the ideas envisaged by those who came before us if they are useful to us?

Since industrialisation **there has been the notion that 'time is money',** or that urban people have no time, and therefore cannot make time to engage directly in producing what they need and offset the costs of their homes, as rural people used to do ... A lot of contemporary problems can be attributed to this wrong assumption. It is now assumed that if we could cut back on the time human beings need to devote to things, then we would be efficient; this eagerness for efficiency overlooks the condition of the human beings in the process, oblivious to whether human society is doing well or not. Standardisation and mass production have led to the undervaluing of human capacities, including intuitive, emotional intelligence and personal judgement, as compared to machine production and operation as the new norm. For all the conveniences and efficiencies achieved, contemporary life is full of stress and rushing about. This also has to do with our notion of time. In order to save time, we have outsourced a lot to machines and increased production and resource consumption dramatically, **while still running out of time for ourselves.**

Despite all the technological advances, contemporary architecture consumes far more resources than that of any previous generation; but are our cities more beautiful, are we happier? **Sustainability,** a key concern of our times, is also **essentially linked to time,** as it focuses on meeting the needs of the present without compromising the ability of future generations to meet *their* needs. It is not only about what materials and technologies are involved in the construction of architecture, but also about the validity and **relevance of contemporary ideas over time.**

Today's rapid urbanisation, with numerous skyscraper cities sprouting across the world at an alarming speed, is redefining the very form of human settlements as high-consumption urban constructs interwoven with informal settlements and with social segregation for the sake of affordability. The commodification of housing and its unaffordability call for alternative approaches, **including the involvement of the time to be spent by future residents** in the way architecture is made and paid for, so that housing can again be perceived as living space rather than as an investment that must necessarily generate huge debts. Reliance on human resources such as time, intelligence, muscle power and direct engagement can reduce the expenditure of natural resources while creating health, wellbeing and happiness.

The tug-of-war between what we call development and the rapidly degrading environment creates a great sense of urgency and panic. Instead of responding to this with equally hasty action, we need **to take the time required to think before we act,** and invest even more time as we may need to radically rethink our future and create new habits that serve our purposes. We can no longer afford to think short-term and for the benefit of the few. In the end our haste only leads to more delay.

Soon after my graduation as an architect from Bombay, with the above preoccupations in my awareness, I decided to take the time I needed to reach clarity about **how to dedicate my time** to the shaping of my own life and my further development as an architect, and how to serve my society while fulfilling myself. During my wanderings I landed in rural Tamil Nadu, where I discovered Auroville, an international city in the making, and quite spontaneously joined in the adventure and started living there, recognizing an exciting opportunity to rethink the city of the future, where human habitation could be realigned holistically as a collective experiment.

As soon as I took the bold decision to drop out of the rat-race environment of Bombay, **I freed up my personal time,** and could finally dedicate substantial **time to doing nothing and contemplating** what is worth doing at all. Taking the time for this doing nothing, I realised that **time was the greatest luxury** for the rich and poor alike. As architects, the work of our lifetime was part of **a large collective action in time and in space.** Contextualising our own journey through time, we can position where we are and how we can contribute. We build upon the work of previous generations in a process of continuous evolution that does not start with our personal existence. This understanding leads to a process where we build knowledge while creating architecture, and addresses the potential of architecture to engage with the complex intersections of urbanisation, people, technologies, resources and the environment within the context of contemporary needs. My practice, the result of my quest for the knowledge needed to build appropriately, considers every project as an opportunity to build knowledge and a sense of community in order to empower people in achieving built spaces of high aesthetic and low environmental impact.

I started observing **the world through the perspective of time.** The passage of time leaves its imprint on the world around us. Even before man existed, architectural constructs existed. In other words, with the passage of time and various circumstances we see the evolution of matter, form, space and order. From sedimentary rocks to volcanic lava, ice formations, boulders shaped by water, etc. the earliest architecture was perhaps about the transformations of matter with the passage of time as it recorded the circumstances that left **the imprint of time on the architecture of matter.** Then there is the imprint time leaves on the **architecture of life** itself. The passage of time and life continues to shape matter by way of other programming that is contained in the DNA of the cells. The architecture of life is expressed through complex order and geometry, where form, space, light and all the key elements of architectural thinking come together synthetically and according to structural principles. The structures of trees and flowers, or mushrooms and shells, networks of arteries and veins whether in animals or in leaves, birds' nests, termite hills, beehives and spiders' webs, continue to inspire architecture for human habitation. Then there is the **architecture of the mind,** where the evolution of the mind and the 'thinking hand' have enabled an architecture where tools were created first, in turn leading to sophisticated developments that have shaped the fabric of architecture accordingly. The building of mud walls evolved through the making of moulds to produce adobe modules which in turn shaped masonry, or, even later, kilns that enabled baking clay modules to be used as baked bricks. The observation of the wondrous world around us as seen through this lens reveals **the architecture of time** to me and continues to be my key inspiration and source of constant learning. One discovers architecture continuously in internal as well as external worlds.

Not only the product of architecture, but the **process of architecture** is of the essence as a living, dynamic and intelligent force that embraces the past, present and future all at once. And the process of architecture is about synthesis. It responds to a diversity of concerns through holistic design definitions. Time is one of the key aspects, the most essential resource that we have access to as living beings. What else do we have that is truly ours apart from our own time? Time is life, and we all have the same number of hours in a day regardless of our geographical context or personal backgrounds. Time well spent enriches us even beyond money, leads to more knowledge and is directly fulfilling; while the stressful urban lives we now accept as normal involve all kinds of detours along the way, making us lose track of the goal, and even contact with ourselves. It makes one wonder that while there is so much eagerness to save money and other resources, **time seems to be an undervalued resource** that is spent in habitual ways rather than wisely or judiciously, and without considering whether such choices are aligned with our purpose or not.

To take time is to be alive. As living beings, the meaning of our lives comes from the way we spend our time. We can reverse the notion that time is running out by getting time on our side, befriending it. We must not race against time, but build a good relationship with the time of our own life. Instead of trying to **make** time, we should **take** time!

Light Housing Prototype, Auroville, India

Light Housing Prototype explores building strategies with a lighter environmental impact in the context of growing concerns about the affordability of housing, and not only in money terms. 'Light' also symbolizes knowledge; and the theme focuses on minimising the 'material' required by using appropriate geometry, form and efficient structural design together with hybrid construction technologies that balance between low-tech and hi-tech. The key strategy for reducing cost, time consumption and material use in the production of houses is to reduce the chief housing component to a lightweight roofing element that minimises the need for columns, beams and walls. The chicken-wire mesh within the ferrocement structure also makes the unit resistant to seismic loads. The roof form is derived from research on origami creasing patterns that give thin paper strength and rigidity. A suitable form is developed according to the proportions suitable for modest human habitation. The module is designed for versatility through combination and repetition in order to arrive at a range of applications for various occupations suitable to members of the household. The module is applicable to a range of contexts such as disaster relief, slum upgrading, temporary housing in sensitive landscapes and youth hostels. Foundations and floor designs depend on site-specific conditions, but in all cases these are efficient as a result of lightweight loads. After initial paper form development exercises, full-scale prototypes were produced in re-used corrugated carton. The selected object was then translated into ferrocement by trying out a range of alternatives for prefabricating the steel mesh elements. The completed prototype was left behind at a residential community, 'Citadines' in Auroville's city centre, where children of the area are now using it as a collective space. The full-scale structure is habitable as an enclosed space which will go beyond fulfilling its role of demonstrating a new approach to lightweight building.

Light Housing Prototype, Auroville, India, 2013
30 m^2

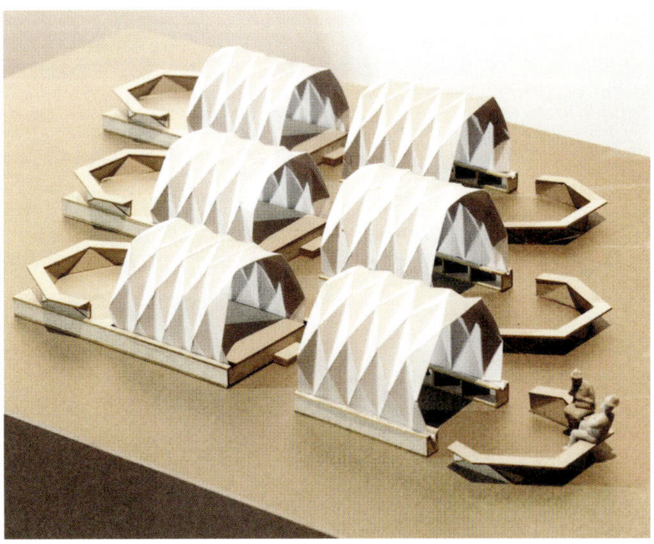

After initial paper form development exercises, full-scale prototypes were produced in re-used corrugated carton.

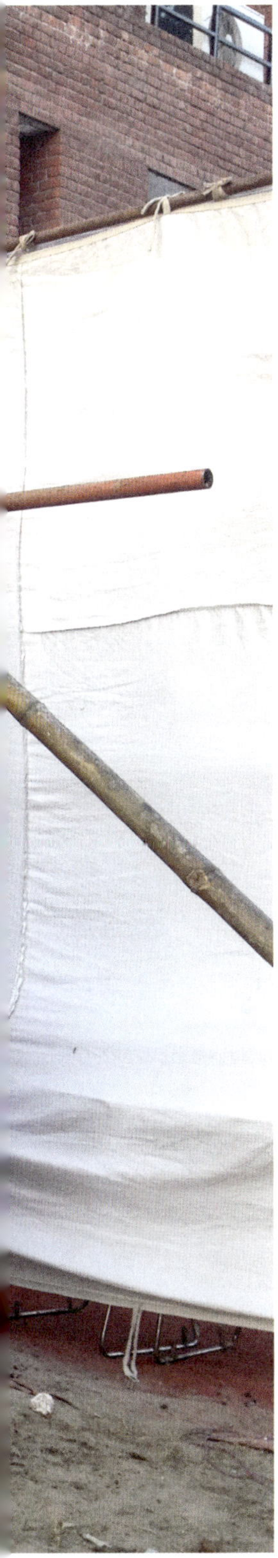

Unbound, The Library of Lost Books, Barcelona, Spain

To express ‘Liberty’ at BCN RE.SET for the 300th anniversary of Catalunya, the pavilion was proposed as a place that celebrates reading and expresses freedom in a place where knowledge is free. An ‘outdoor’ place under the shade of ‘trees’, where everybody has a memory of reading books, the pavilion is free from the confines of walls of buildings. Books, ‘the building blocks’ of society, may be facing extinction. However, the act of ‘reading’ continues. ‘Obsolete’ books locked in storage, about to face their end, are recycled as construction material to for building a canopy. Books made at the environmental cost of trees are recycled and reconstructed into trees to create an open-air reading space, a bookless library that focuses on the act of reading rather than the storage of books which are objects in transition. Three canopies shade the Salvador Seguí Square through central trunks constructed of steel tubular profiles of varying diameters just like branches. Smaller-diameter tubes penetrate the larger-diameter ones which lean outwards, progressively creating a large overhang. The canopies are made of vacuum-packed books, packaged the same way as delicatessen items like ham and olives, to symbolise the extension of shelf life and create the association of being highly valued though familiar association. These are assembled and attached to the structure using cable wire.

Unbound, The Library of Lost Books, 2014
BCN RE.SET, Barcelona, Spain
150 m^2

Anupama Kundoo during the opening in conversation with Odile Secq, while curator Benedetta Tagliabue looks on (p. 169).

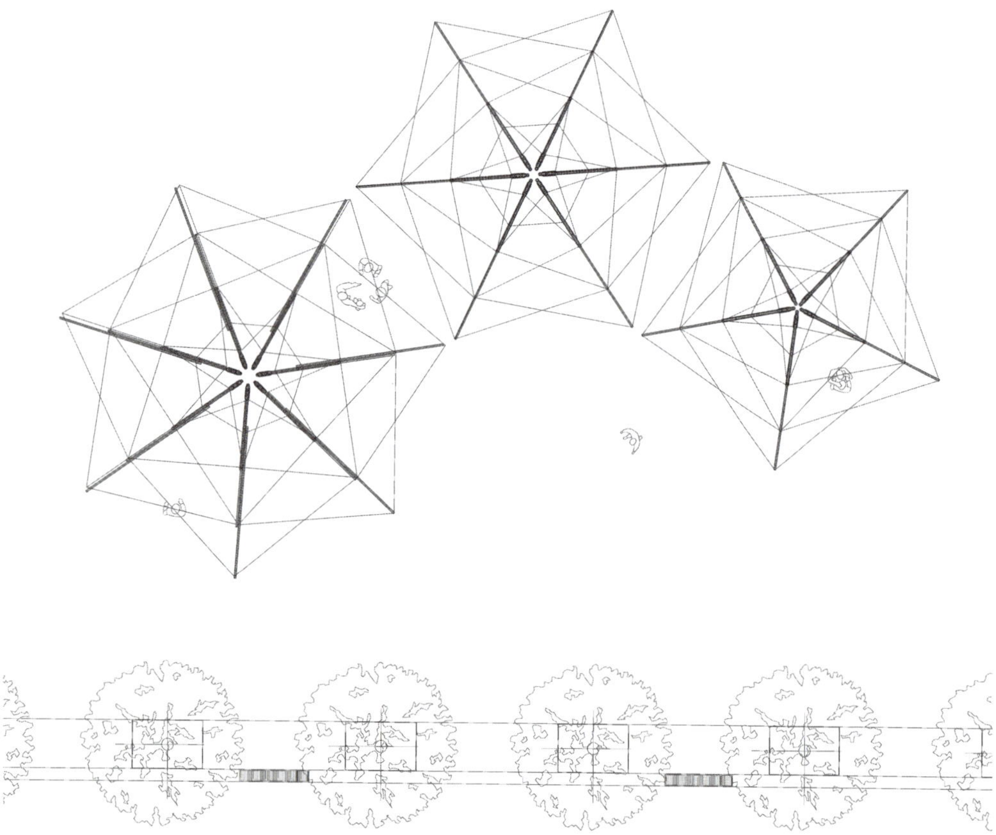

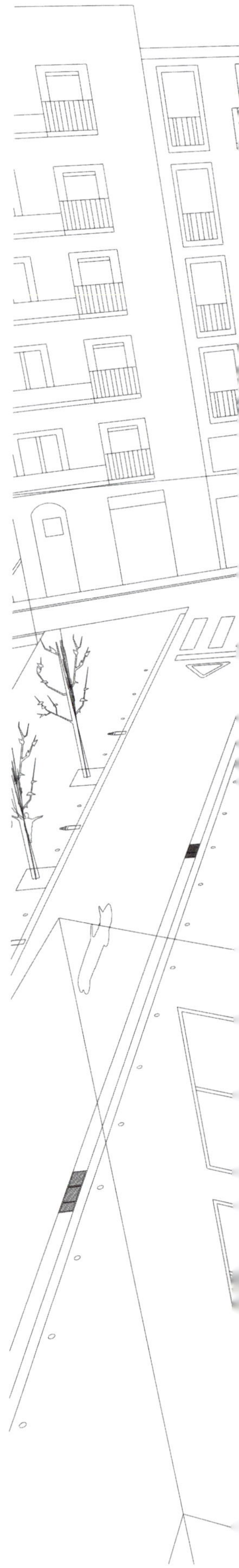

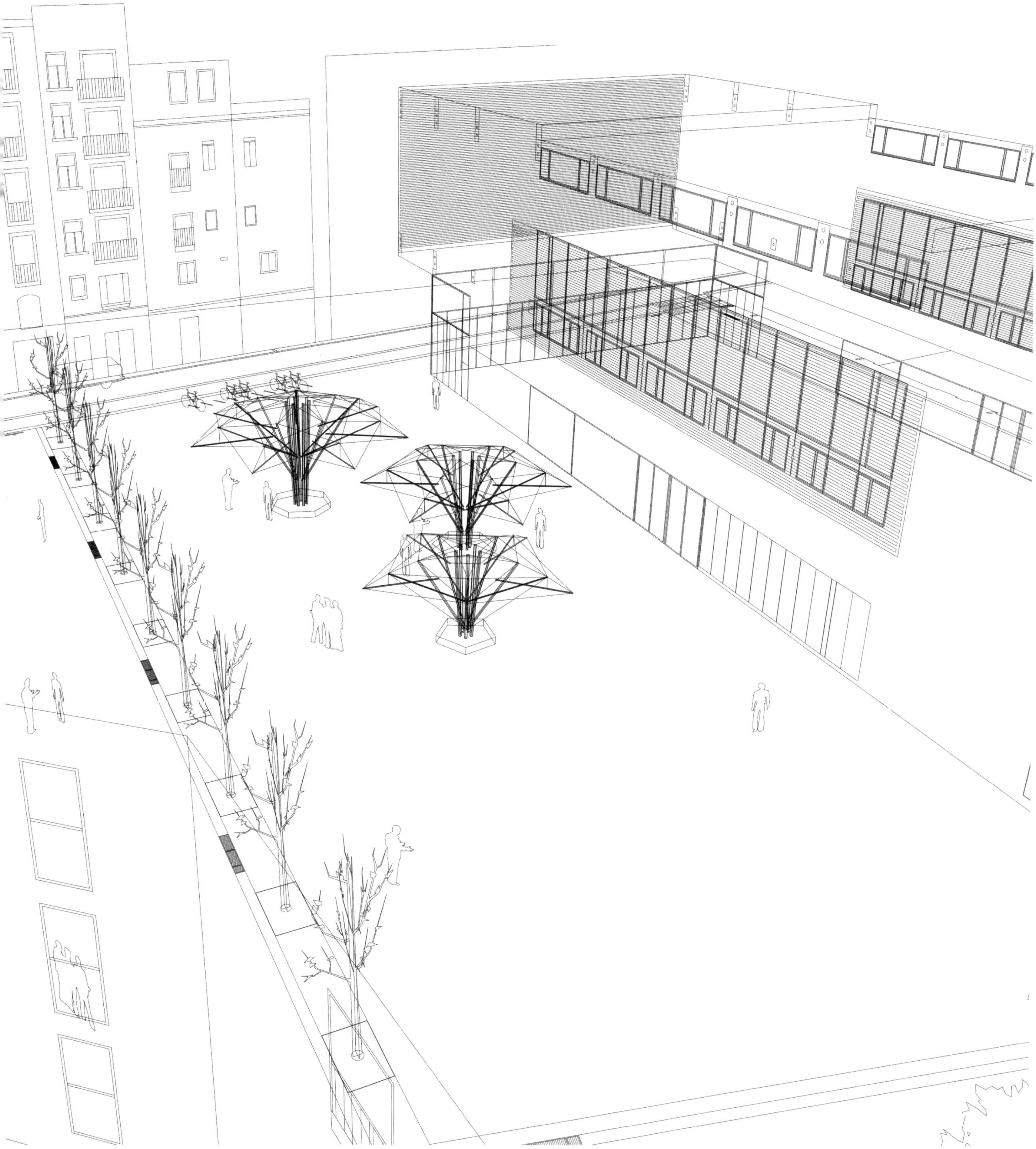

Library Nandalal Sewa Samithi, Pondicherry, India

Set in a residential area of rapidly urbanising Pondicherry, the new library building is realised as a social infrastructure facilitated through the social organisation Nandalal Sewa Samithi. Affordability being a key consideration, the library is a construction built in locally made, exposed bricks, which would stand out as an institutional building in the context of the plastered and painted masonry construction of the surrounding houses and apartment buildings. The roof profile represents the 'open book', as do the screening elements conceived in ferrocement technology symbolising constant progress through knowledge. The orthogonal walls on the upper floor lean outwards towards the top like a crown, as the building aims to serve the community and invest in its empowerment by encouraging reading and learning. As land is limited by the residential plot sizes, the terrace upstairs is designed to compensate for this by providing the necessary open space for contemplation and informal outdoor events. The inclusiveness of this facility is demonstrated by the inclusion of Braille books for the visually impaired. This particular feature is reflected architecturally in the way a Braille typeface is integrated into the building elements to create porous patterns in the brickwork, screens and ceiling. Light patterns in the form of Braille texts leave their imprint on the interior spaces so that those who can see are visually aware of the language of those who cannot see, and thus increase their sensitivity to the differently abled.

Library Nandalal Sewa Samithi, 2018
Pondicherry, India
268 m²

The roof terrace upstairs is designed to compensate for the lack of public spaces for contemplation and informal outdoor events.

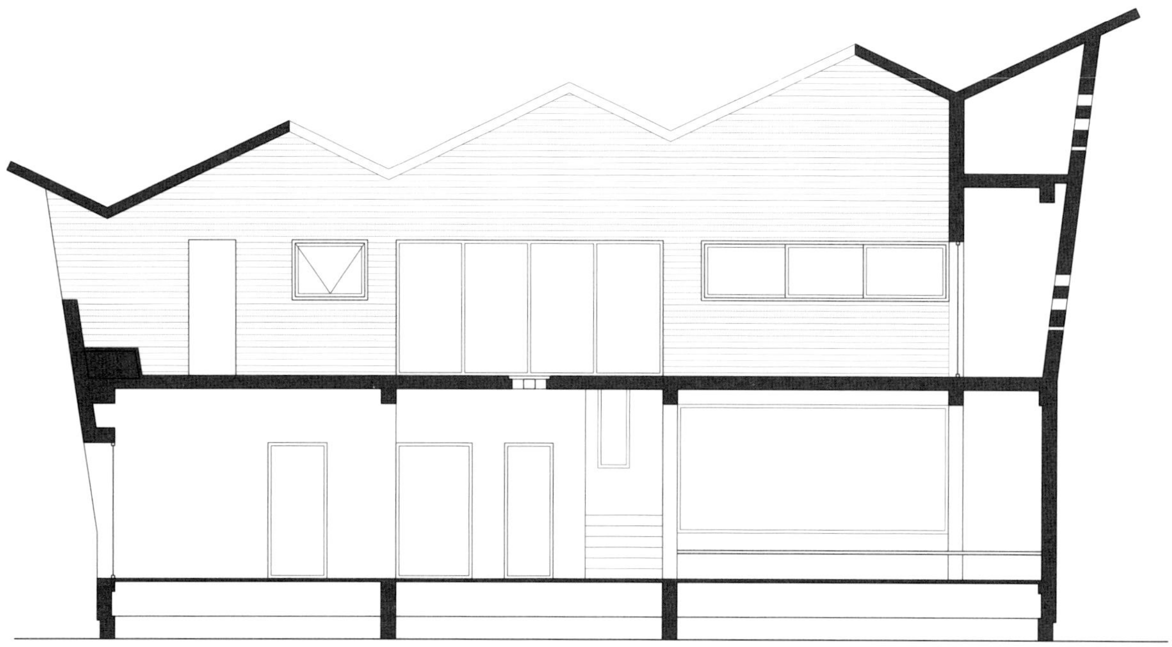

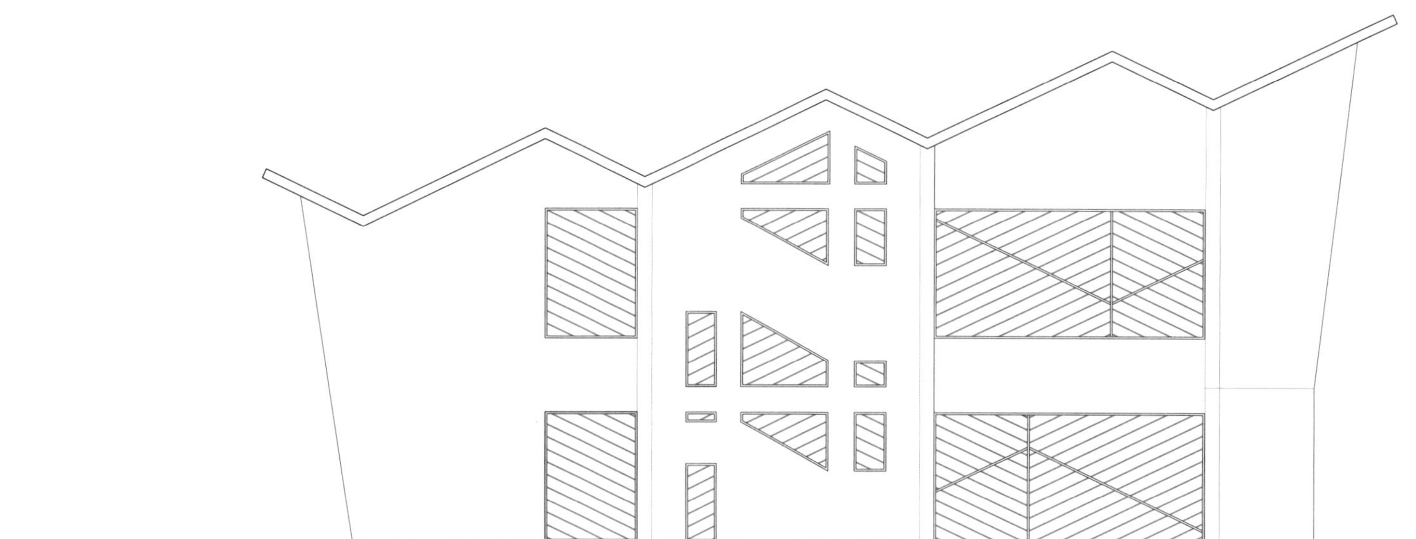

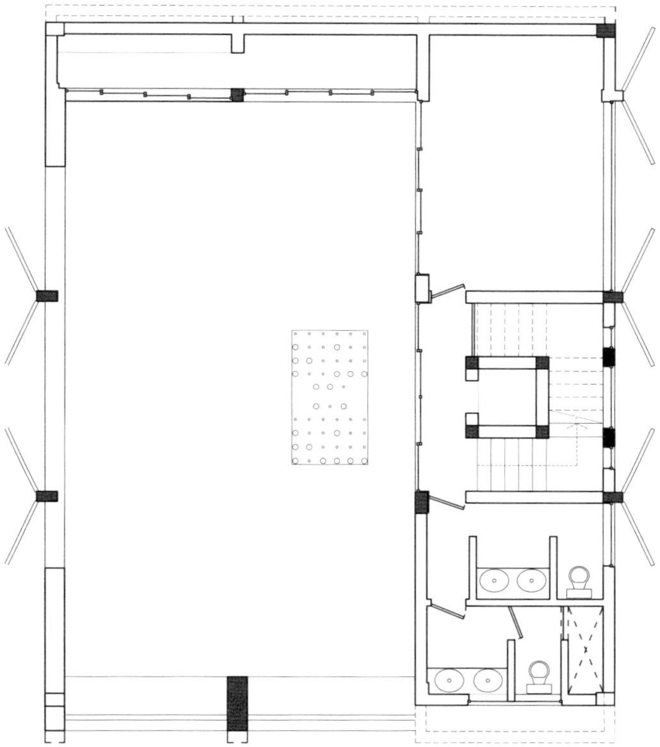

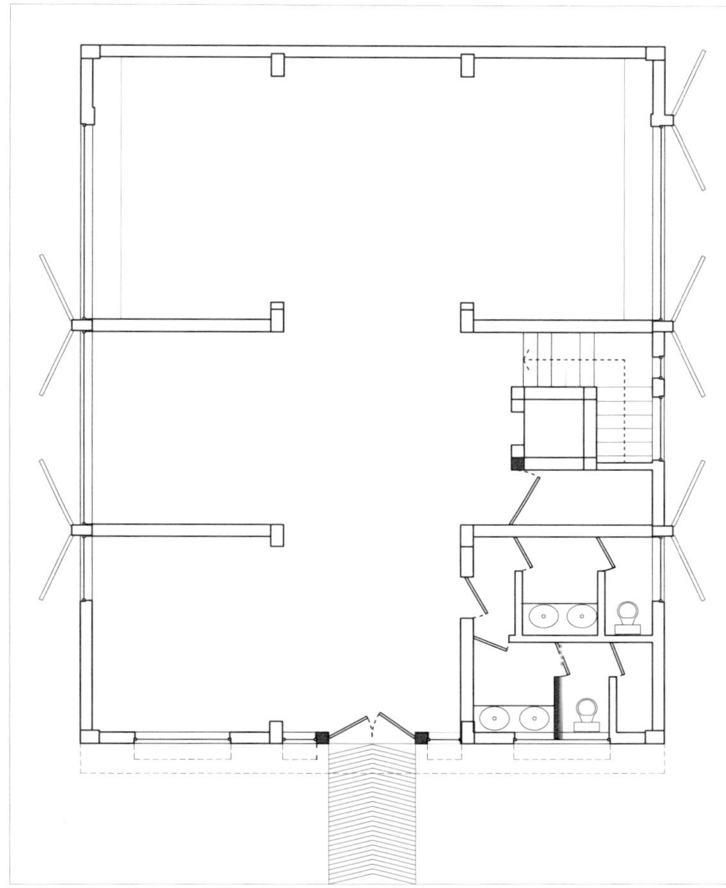

Science & Technology Arts & Recreation
Computer Science
3
E
E
F
4
G
G
H
ENGLISH
WAY TO MEDITATION HALL

As the library also houses books in Braille, the architecture includes Braille script patterns to source light in the interiors and sensitise users who can see to the presence of the visually challenged.

Full Fill Homes, Auroville, India

In response to growing homelessness, Full Fill Homes is envisaged as a speedy and affordable housing-unit prototype of low environmental impact that promotes self-building knowledge and community empowerment. A Full Fill Homes unit, which can be assembled on site in seven days including foundation work, relies on structural ingenuity to achieve innovative high-speed, lightweight construction. The 25 mm ferrocement elements rely on small quantities of easily available materials: chicken mesh replaces steel bars, mortar replaces concrete. This reduces energy in the production process and transport; avoids industrial finishing materials; incorporates water-efficient fabrication and curing; and demonstrates superior ductile properties against seismic forces which are a growing concern due to climate change. The folded box-shaped forms, a structural necessity for strengthening the very thin elements, double up to achieve ergonomically designed voids, which become the complete storage solution for the homeowners, accommodating clothes, books, kitchen utensils, even the kitchen sink and personal belongings, making furniture redundant and rooms spacious. Bright happy colours accentuate and define the void spaces thanks to coloured oxides embedded in the cement slurry. This eliminates the need for finishing materials and gives cement surfaces a polished, waxed surface that is waterproof and easy to maintain. As a social-sustainability strategy, the modular blocks are produced in the back yards of masons' homes in nearby villages as an innovative co-production concept, rather than in factories, providing masons with additional income as entrepreneurs, permitting flexible timing, encouraging the participation of women and reducing costs while helping the local economy and promoting the natural dissemination of knowledge. Windows, doors, roof elements and other necessary building components are all produced in ferrocement, excluding any complex hardware in their design.

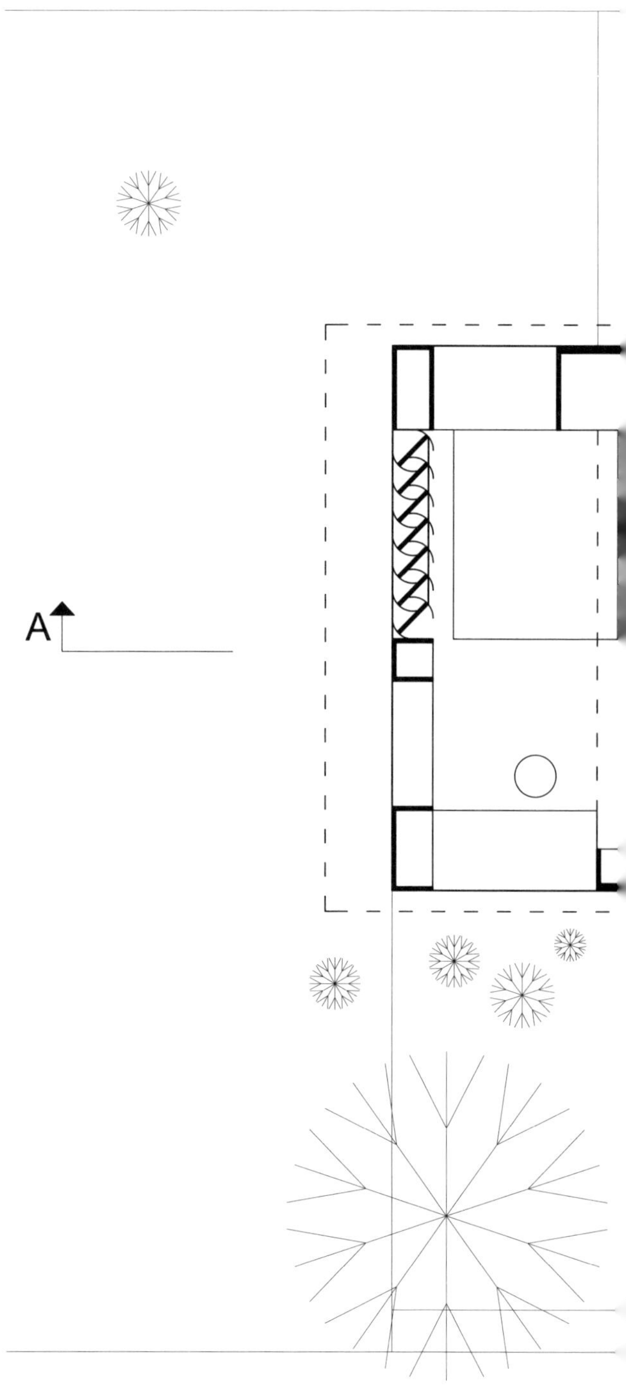

Full Fill Homes, 2015
Auroville, India
30 m^2

B
A'

Step 1

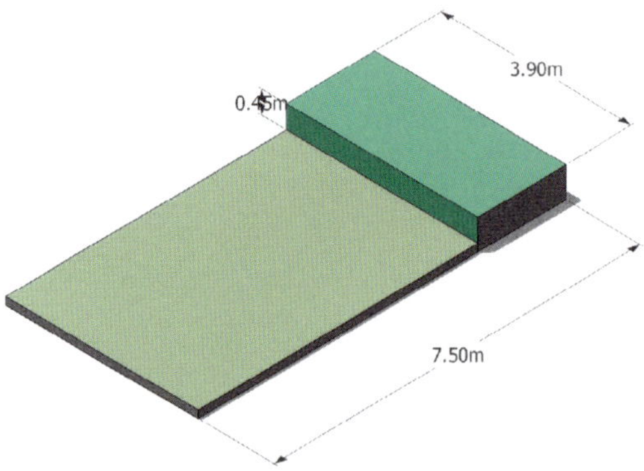

Step 2

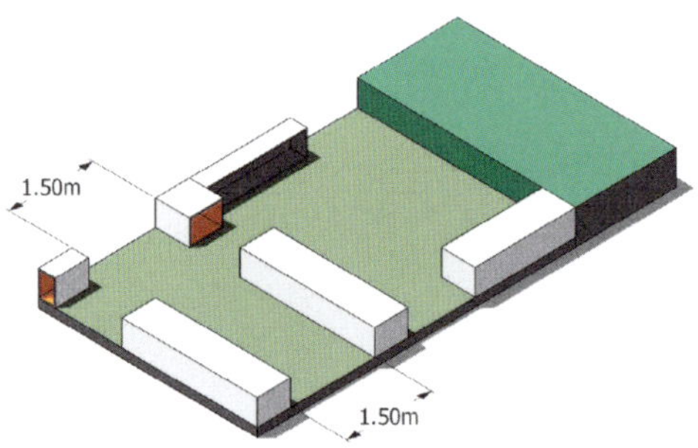

Step 3

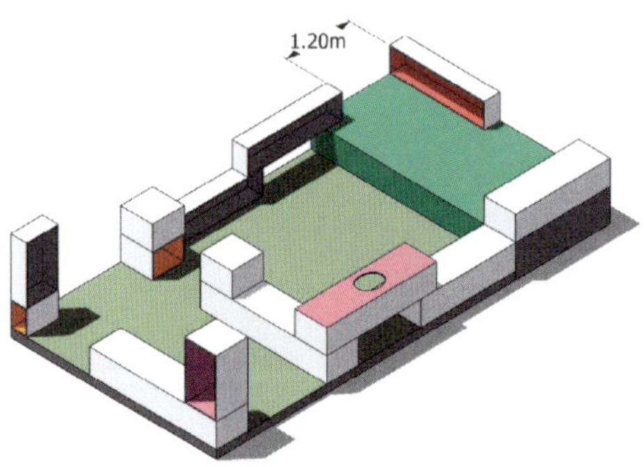

Step 4

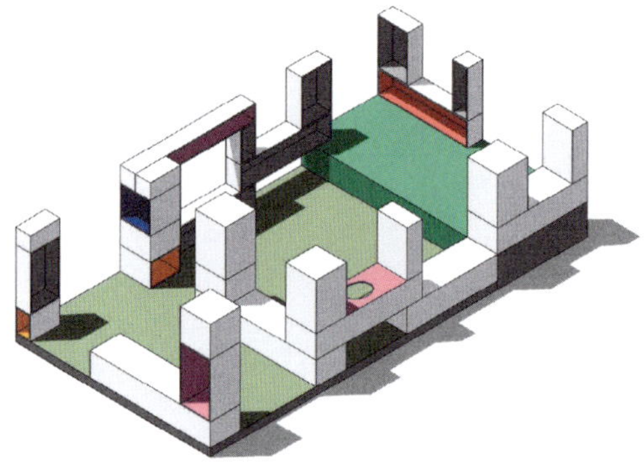

Step 5

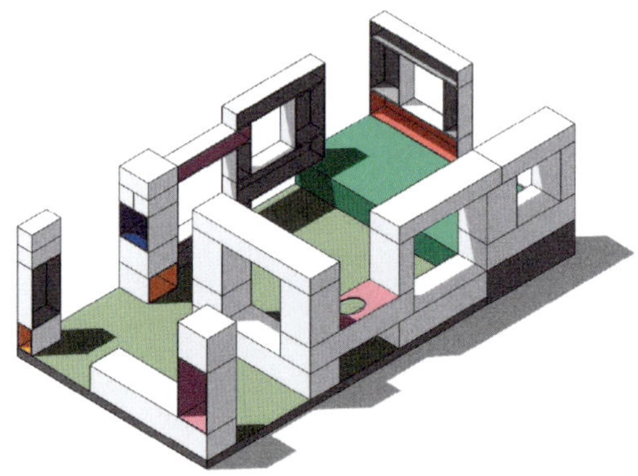

Step 6

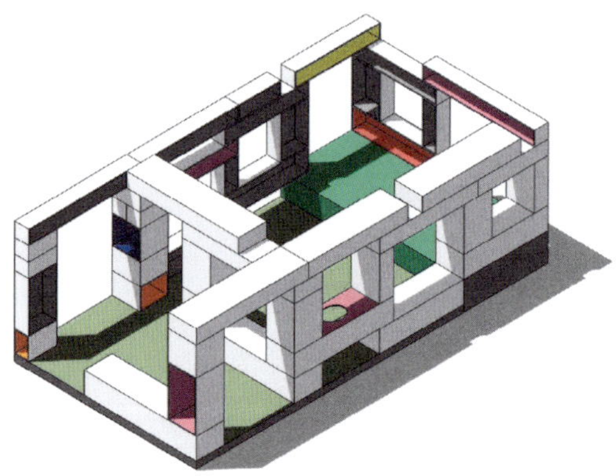

Full Fill Homes built at the Venice Biennale of Architecture, 2016.

FERROCEMENT WITH
HEXAGONAL MESH,
GALVANIZED Ø 0,7 mm

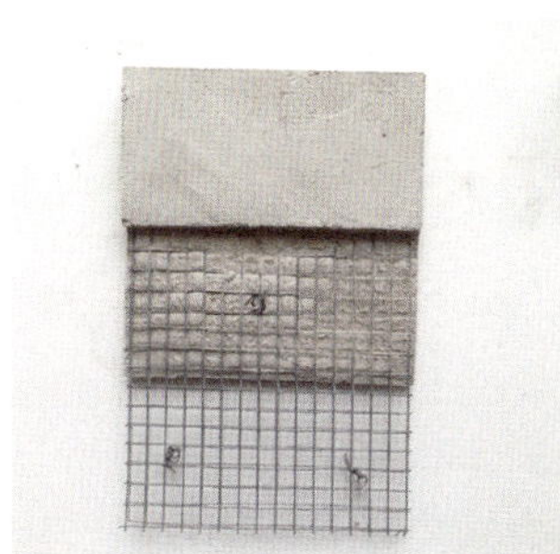

The 25 mm thick ferrocement elements used chicken mesh, welded mesh and small-diameter steel reinforcement, significantly reducing the quantity of high-embodied-energy materials used in the construction.

In an interdisciplinary workshop conducted by Kundoo in collaboration with Professor Mike Schlaich and Arndt Goldack of T.U. Berlin in 2016, Indian masons, alongside German engineers, produced ferrocement elements. These elements were later load-tested, and exhibited higher strength and ductile properties than expected.

Affordability is due to efficiency and inclusivity. The design is versatile and can serve as immediate shelters, urban as well as remote areas, disaster relief homes, youth hostels, student housing or plugged into high-rise construction frameworks. These versatile elements can be dismantled in a day, reassembled in various configurations or even shifted elsewhere. Furniture costs are saved too. The Easy WC combines a shower and toilet cubicle on either side of a covered platform with a washbasin. The base plate can be plugged into different sanitation systems: septic tank, dry toilet pit or collective drainage system.

Sharana Daycare Facility, Pondicherry, India

Sharana is a social and development organization established to address the critical educational needs of socioeconomically disadvantaged children and communities in urban Pondicherry and its surrounding villages. Sharana's foundational belief is that all human beings are equal in rights and dignity, and everyone is entitled to food, clothing and shelter. The architecture revolves around the central strip of an inner garden court with large multipurpose activity spaces at the rear of the site, and reception/administration services at the front on the street. The building is constructed as reinforced cement concrete slabs on columns of the same material. To enclose the various spaces economically, walls are made of porous terracotta screen modules that can be quickly erected and eliminate the need for windows and frames while allowing ventilation throughout the wall surface, economically achieving the required conditions for climatic comfort in the tropical context. These screen wall elements allow transparency from the floor upwards, allowing small children to remain in visual contact with the garden outdoors. The porous elements express transparency and inclusiveness as per the aims of the institute, and in practice require no additional finishes like plasters and paint as in regular masonry, while also minimizing maintenance. In order to give the activity rooms their own identity and sense of enclosure, and to break the monotony of long corridors, the geometry of angular walls as composition elements is the ordering principle. This feature gives the corridor and entrance areas a sense of enclosure, identity and a sense of intimacy appropriate to the scale of small children, and helps them with orientation within the complex, completely deconstructing the impression of long monotonous corridors.

Sharana Daycare Facility, 2019
Pondicherry, India
766 m²

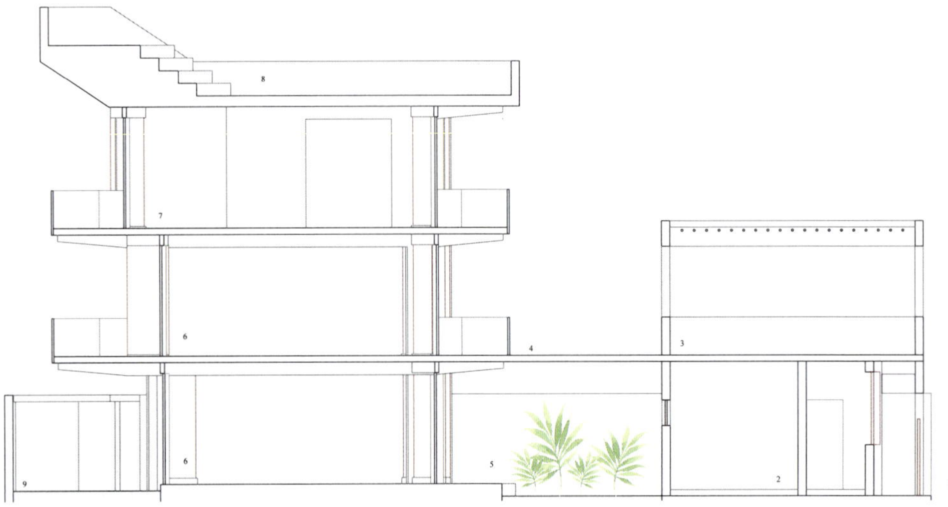
8
7
6
4
3
6
5
2
1
9

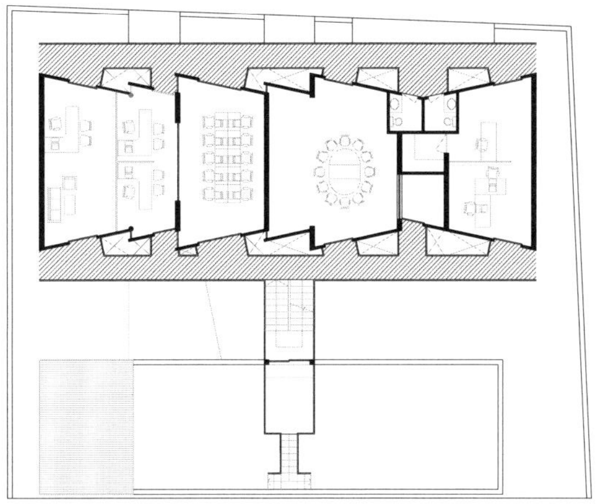

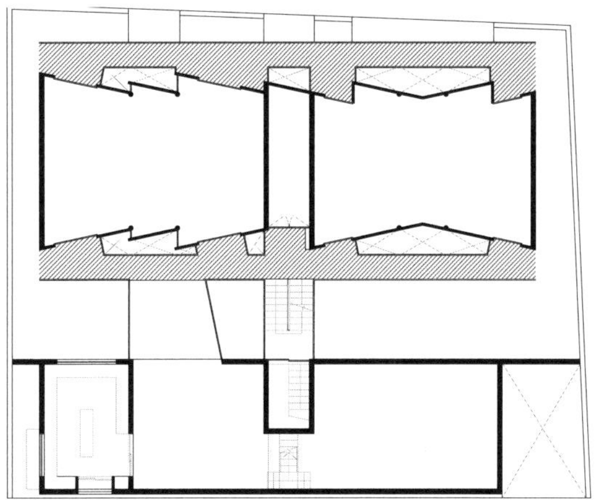

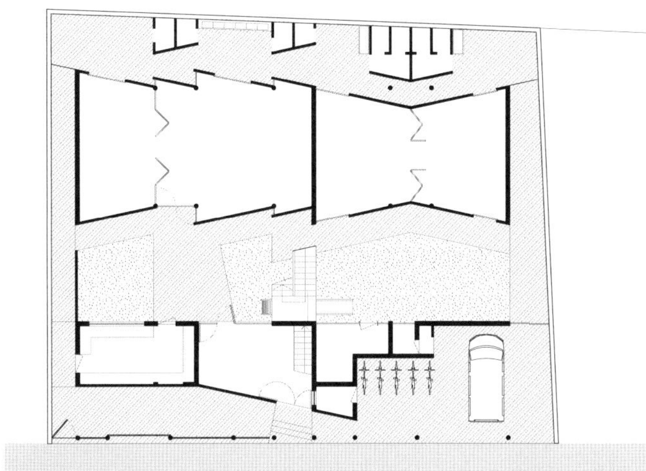

To enclose the various spaces economically, walls are made of porous terracotta screen modules that are speedy to erect and eliminate the need for windows and frames while allowing ventilation throughout the wall surface.

Line of Goodwill

By Anupama Kundoo

The Auroville Background

In 1965, Mirra Alfassa, also known as The Mother, the spiritual partner of Aurobindi Ghose, one of the leading freedom fighters in India, envisaged a new city, Auroville, named after Sri Aurobindo and dedicated to achieving human unity and international understanding based on a vision that “somewhere on earth there should be a place which no nation can claim as its own, where all human beings of good will who have sincere aspirations can live freely as citizens of the world ...” In 1965, The Mother invited French architect Roger Anger (1923-2008), one of the most prolific architects in Paris in the 1950s and 1960s, to design the city. His unique architectural language was characterized by sculptural plasticity and individualized, timeless modernity. On 28 February 1968 the foundation of this city was laid 10 km north of Pondicherry in a barren ‘wasteland’ with the participation of 5,000 people from 125 countries and all the Indian states, bringing a handful of earth from their homelands to a marble-clad urn in the shape of a lotus bud that still stands at the centre of this planned city.

Auroville began with a four-point charter:

1. Auroville belongs to nobody in particular. Auroville belongs to humanity as a whole. But to live in Auroville, one must be a willing servitor of the divine consciousness.
2. Auroville will be the place for unending education, constant progress, and a youth that never ages.
3. Auroville wants to be the bridge between the past and the future. Taking advantage of all discoveries from without and from within, Auroville will leap boldly towards future realizations.
4. Auroville will be a site for material and spiritual research towards a living embodiment of true human unity.

The city plan is a "galaxy concept", an arrangement of four principal areas - residential, industrial, cultural and international - in a radiating, spirally rotating movement around the city centre. The gradual integration of and communication among the zones is facilitated by a rotating circular plan which makes them less segregated and more interwoven, to merge completely at the city centre as a unified whole around an oval island with a central building called 'Matrimandir' representing the soul of this city.

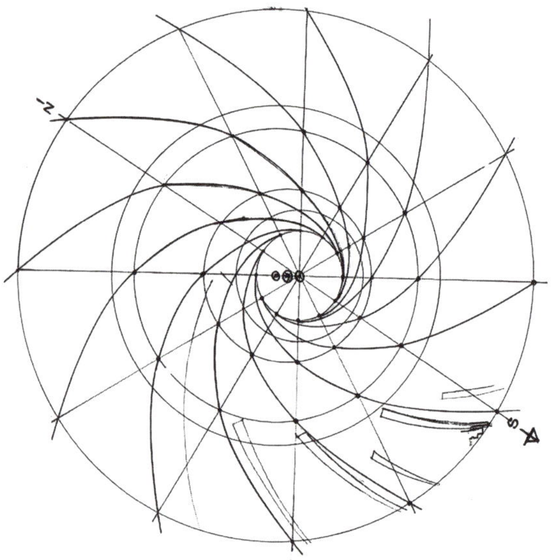

Old Last School, Roger Anger, 1971

Sanskrit School, Roger Anger, 1971. Originally named After School 1, this school is a sculptural expression of free forms arranged around a courtyard.

Bottom: Matrimandir, Roger Anger, 1971-2008. A pattern of golden discs form the outer-skin of the building, over ferrocement elements that cover the triangular structural framework.

The collaboration with Roger Anger

Anupama Kundoo began her practice in Auroville in 1990. From an early stage she began collaborating with Roger Anger, chief architect of Auroville, but became more involved from 1996 onward when Anger gave her more tasks. She collaborated with him on Bharat Nivas, Indian Pavilion Campus 1998, and was part of the team that produced Auroville's Masterplan Perspective 2025 in 1999, approved by the Ministry of Human Resource Development in 2001. Following this she produced proposals for Auroville Administrative Zone 2002, Habitat Belt and Auroville City Centre 2007 under his supervision. She began studies for the high-density structure in 2002 and continued the work after his passing in 2008. In 2009 she authored the first monograph on Roger Anger, *Research on Beauty*.

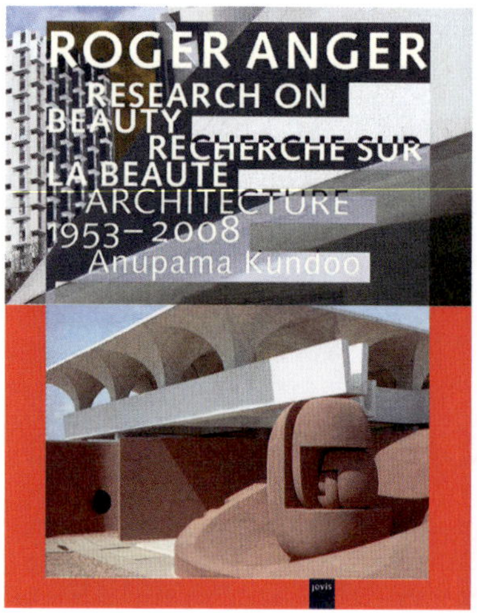

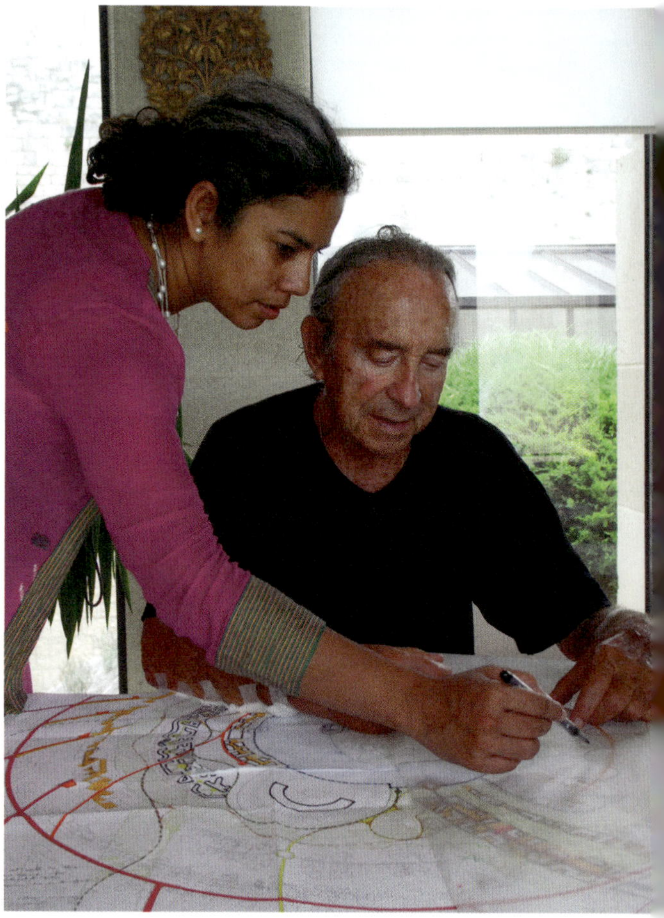

In 2015, Kundoo produced an Urban Design Proposal for Line10, one of the high-density structures of Auroville's Masterplan in the eastern part of the Resident Zone. The quest for a new prototype for high-density collective living was envisaged in the context of a car-free future city with a continuous green network that radiates from the garden-like city centre.

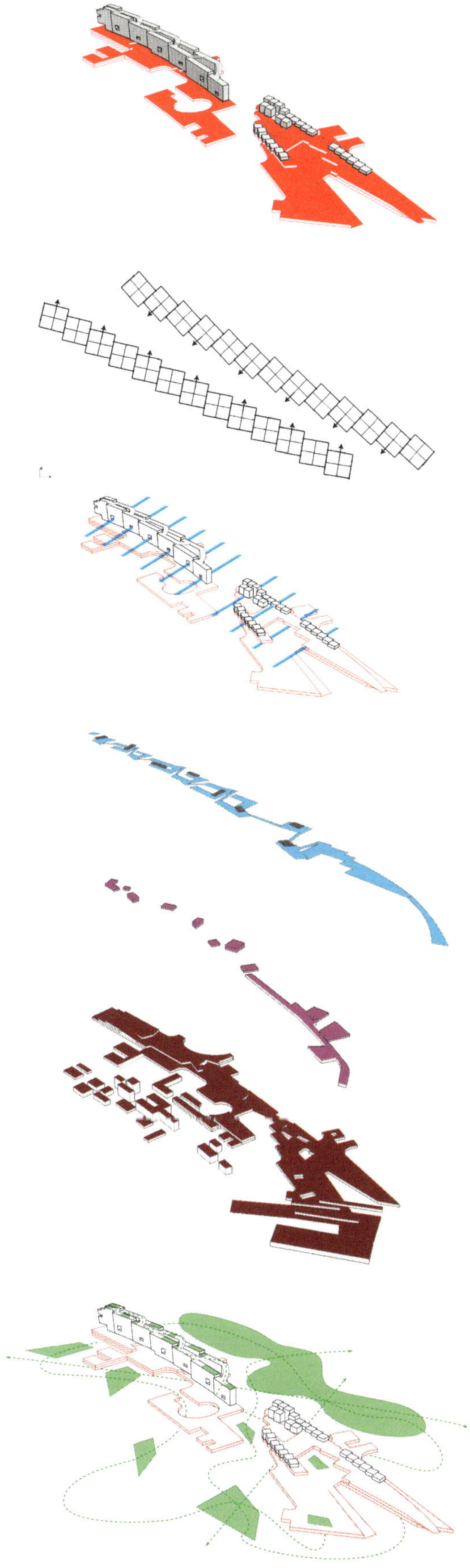

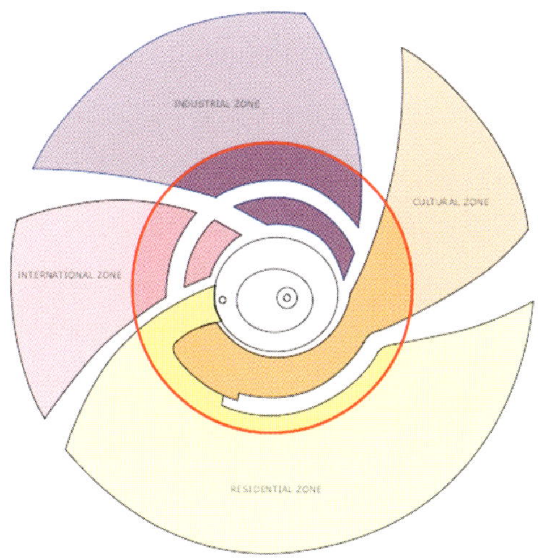

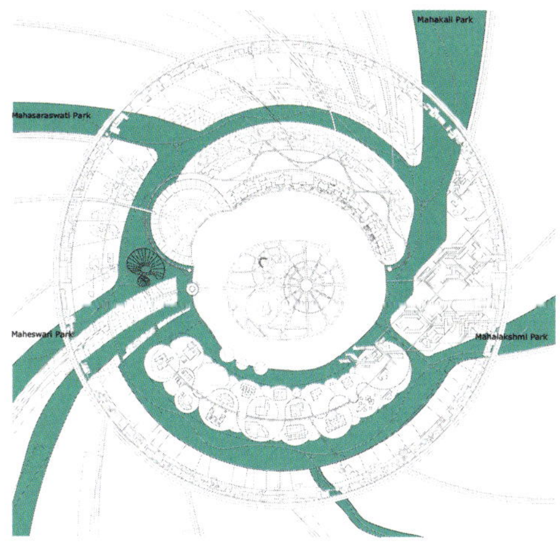

Line of Goodwill, Auroville, India

Planned as an urban project of co-housing clusters, the Line of Goodwill is the first high-density compact housing envisaged for Auroville so it can take a bold urban step, 50 years after its foundation, in the direction of the compact pedestrian city planned by its chief architect Roger Anger. To compensate for the low-rise housing in the green city of Auroville, and still provide the required compactness and density, Anger introduced urban structures that he called *Lignes de Force*. These extremely long porous structures rise tall above the rest of the city at one end, and gradually slope down over the entire length to reach the ground at its other end. In the residential zone, the towering heights are located towards the periphery of the city, their terraces facing the city centre. These structures enhance the dynamic spiralling movement of the town plan and absorb density with a minimum of circulation on the ground through vertical development. The cluster of buildings stretching over 800 metres starts at the entrance to the city, as a gateway for visitors, including hotel facilities with an 18-storey height radially descending towards the city centre and reaching the edge of the central lake. It accommodates 8,000 inhabitants and includes the first steps towards a public transportation system. The large scale of the project allows radical and integral rethinking of habitat, including social, environmental and economic aspects: the creation of vibrant street life for spontaneous exchanges in public space at upper levels, the aim of addressing the human scale, intimacy and well-being despite the high-rise context increased opportunities to share chores and childcare, freeing up personal time for improving the quality of human life beyond ownership of land or assets, establishing a sense of

Line of Goodwill, 2017 onwards
Auroville, India
240,000 m^2

UNITY PAVILION
SAVITRI BHAVAN
MATRIMANDIR
LAKE
KINDERGARTENS
CULTURAL ZONE
NANDANAM SCHOOL
AUROVILLE CENTER
GUEST HOUSE
RESIDENTIAL ZONE
PTDC
SOLAR KITCHEN
CROWN BUILDING

the common opportunities for participation in the construction as a collective process, the development of appropriate building technologies for high-rises with local materials and skills that boost the local economy while reducing embodied energy and pollution with a heightened awareness of the impact on health alternative strategies for debt financing through a circular economy pedestrian-centric urban development with mixed use and proximity to places of work, recreation and social infrastructure, with connections to collectively owned bicycles and non-polluting vehicles integral management of water and waste water, from direct re-use to irrigation solar passive principles for climatic comfort 'no-waste' management of daily life including integration of onsite compost production; prevention of noise pollution including during construction integration of urban farming opportunities on roofs and facades along with the related irrigation systems.

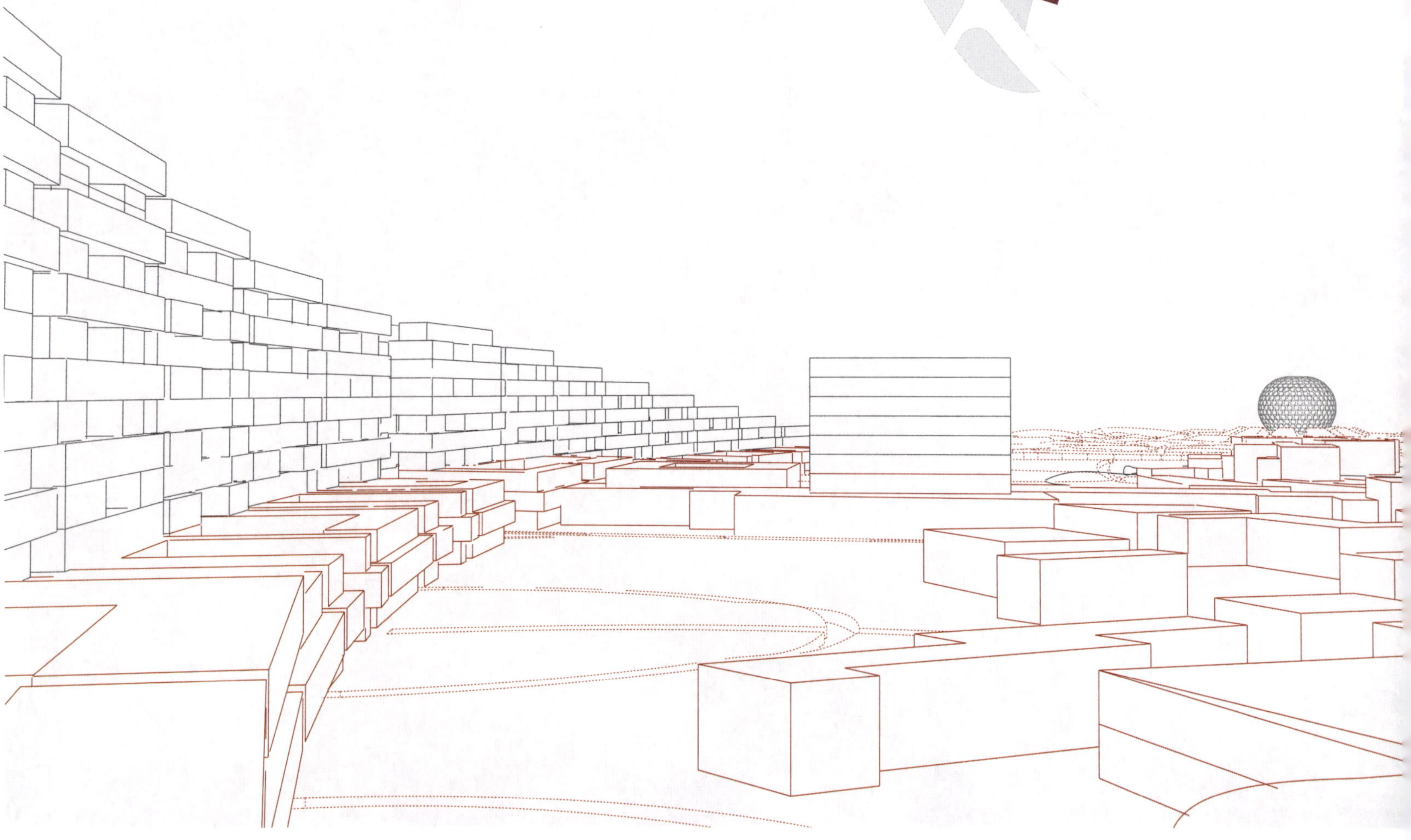

Today Kundoo is working continuously, in collaboration with Ratan J. Batliboi Architects and 28 students from various universities around the globe, on the development and realization of Line of Goodwill.

The large scale of the project allows radical and integral rethinking of habitat, and these include social, environmental and economic aspects:

- creation of a vibrant street life for spontaneous exchanges at public space at upper levels
- the quest for addressing human scale, intimacy and well-being despite the high rise context
- increased opportunities to share chores and childcare, liberating personal time for improving the quality of human life
- beyond ownership of land or assets and establishing a sense of the commons opportunities for participation in the construction as a collective process
- development of appropriate building technologies for high rise with local materials and skills boosting local economy, while reducing embodied energy and pollution and awareness of impact on health
- alternative strategies to debt financing through circular economy
- pedestrian centric urban development with mixed use and proximity to places of work, recreation and social infrastructure, with connections to collectively owned bicycles and non-polluting vehicles
- integral management of water and waste water, from direct reuse to irrigation
- solar passive principles for climatic comfort
- 'no-waste' management of daily life including integration of onsite compost production; prevention of noise pollution including during construction
- integration of urban farming opportunities on roofs and facades along with the related irrigation systems.

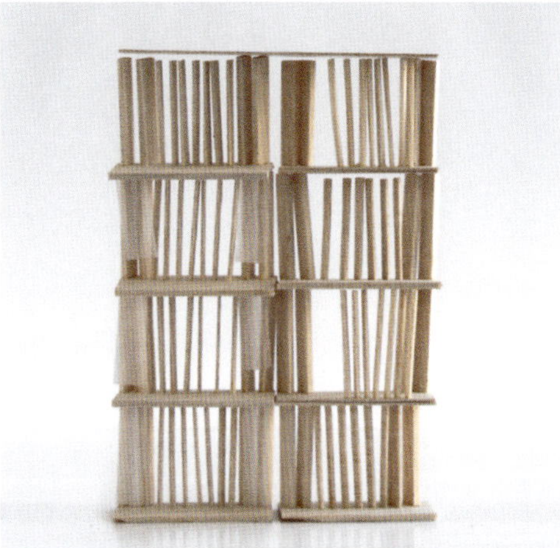

Facade proposals from the workshop 'Rethinking Housing: mediating transitions between the individual and public scale', KADK, Copenhagen, 2018.

Anupama Kundoo's Acknowledgements

Principal collaborating architects in Anupama Kundoo's team: Sonali Phadnis, Yashoda Joshi

Assistance towards catalogue: Luna Bucherer

Photography of Anupama Kundoo's early years as an architect: Andreas Deffner

Hand drawings on p. 35, 44-45, 112-113: Alejandro Martinez del Rio

Institutional collaborations: Fachhochschule, Potsdam; Yale University, New Haven; Universität Stuttgart; KADK, Copenhagen; ENSA, Nantes; IE School of Architecture and Design, Madrid/ Segovia; UCJC, Madrid; IAAC, Barcelona; ETSAB, Barcelona; University of Queensland, Brisbane; Cornell University, Ithaca; IUAV, Venice; Parsons The New School of Design, New York; Architectural Association, London; Sir J.J. College of Architecture, Mumbai; Technische Universität, Berlin

Interdisciplinary collaborations: Ray Meeker, R. Ambalavanan, Venkata Rangarao, Zarna Barday, Ranjit Ghatge, Puruchottamane, Prof. Dr. Mike Schlaich, Prof. Dr. Arndt Goldack, Ratan J Batliboi Consultants, Ingenieurbüro Kraft Beratende Ingenieure für Wasserwirtschaft, Transsolar KlimaEngineering

Construction firms: Saminathan, Sumark Constructions, Aryan Builders, Auronirmata Constructions, M. Vinayagam, Narasimman S., Creations, Vilasware Constructions, Sanjay Deshpande, Sriram Contractors

The Architect's Studio

Anupama Kundoo

Edited by Mette Marie Kallehauge and Lærke Rydal Jørgensen

Graphic Design: Camilla Jørgensen and Søren Damstedt, Trefold
Translation from the Danish: Glen Garner (foreword)
Proofreading: James Manley
Desk Editor: Pernille G. Johansson
Front Cover and Endpapers: Anupama Kundoo, Wall House, Auroville, India, 2000. Photo: Javier Callejas

Litho: Narayana Press
Print: Narayana Press
ISBN Louisiana Museum of Modern Art: 978-87-93659-33-9
ISBN Lars Müller Publishers: 978-3-03778-637-6
Printed in Denmark 2020

Lars Müller Publishers is supported by the Swiss Federal Office of Culture with a structural contribution for the years 2016–2020.

Lars Müller Publishers
Zürich, Switzerland
www.lars-mueller-publishers.com

Louisiana Museum of Modern Art
Humlebæk, Denmark
www.louisiana.dk

Distributed in North America by ARTBOOK | D.A.P.
www.artbook.com

This catalogue is published on the occasion of the exhibition
The Architects Studio
Anupama Kundoo – Taking Time
Louisiana Museum of Modern Art 8 October 2020 – 31 January 2021

Curators: Kjeld Kjeldsen and Mette Marie Kallehauge
Curatorial Coordinator: Marianne Ahrensberg
Exhibition Producer and Conservator: Mikkel Storch
Architect: Brian Lottenburger
Assistant: Amalie Rosenkrantz Hölmich
Graphic Design: Marie d'Origny Lübecker and Thomas Joakim Winther

Photo:
All photos: © Javier Callejas. Except for © Andreas Deffner: p. 12-15, 20-23, 26, 28-31, 36, 37, 46, 49, 53, 74,110, 192, 194, 231; © Anupama Kundoo: p. 16 (bottom), 17 (bottom), 146, 156-59, 164-65, 192 (top), 193, 196; © Roberto Conte: p. 17 (top); © Alka Hingorani: p. 19 (bottom), 60-64; © Andreas Herzog: p. 65; © Sonja Winkler: p. 66, 67, 69 (bottom), 71 (top right, middle right), 72 (top), © Marta San Vicente: p. 160 (top), 161-63; © Blas Llamazares: p. 195; © Sebastiano Giannesini: p. 197; © Dominique Darr: p. 216, 217, 218; © Ariadna A. Garreta: p. 218, 219-221; © Anne Pind: p. 222 (bottom); © Alba Balmaseda: p. 227 (top), 229; © Joel Brynielsson: p. 228

All drawings: © Anupama Kundoo Architects. Except for © Alejandro Martinez del Rio: p. 35, 44-45, 112-113; © Estate of Roger Anger: p. 214, 218 (bottom)

The exhibition is supported by

Realdania

Sponsor of Louisiana's architectural exhibitions